THE ELEMENT GUIDE

BEREAVEMENT

Ursula Markham has been a hypnotherapist and counsellor for the past 16 years, during which she has spent a great deal of time in bereavement counselling and helping patients to cope with losses of all types – from suicide to child death, terminal illness to sudden widowhood. She is also an extremely experienced and successful author and has written numerous books on self-help subjects.

THE ELEMENT GUIDE SERIES

The Element Guide series provides clear, practical advice on psychological and emotional states to bring help and guidance to sufferers and their families.

In the same series

Anorexia & Bulimia by Julia Buckroyd
Anxiety, Phobias and Panic Attacks by Elaine Sheehan
Depression by Sue Breton

• THE ELEMENT GUIDE •

BEREAVEMENT

Your Questions Answered

Ursula Markham

ELEMENT

Shaftesbury, Dorset • Rockport, Massachusetts
Brisbane, Queensland

© Ursula Markham 1996

First published in Great Britain in 1996 by
Element Books Limited
Shaftesbury, Dorset SP7 8BP

Published in the USA in 1996 by
Element Books, Inc.
PO Box 830, Rockport, MA 01966

Published in Australia in 1996 by
Element Books Limited
for Jacaranda Wiley Limited
33 Park Road, Milton, Brisbane 4064

Cover design by Max Fairbrother
Page design by Roger Lightfoot
Typeset by Footnote Graphics, Warminster, Wiltshire
Printed and bound in Great Britain by Biddles Ltd,
Guildford & King's Lynn

British Library Cataloguing in Publication
data available

Library of Congress Cataloging in Publication
data available

ISBN 1–85230–774–9

Note from the Publisher
Any information given in any book in the *Element Guide* series is not
intended to be taken as a replacement for medical advice. Any person
with a condition requiring medical attention should consult a qualified
medical practitioner or suitable therapist.

Contents

To Philip and David
With all my love

Think then, my soul, that death is but a groom
Which brings a taper to the outward room

'Of the Progress of the Soul'
John Donne (1572–1631)

Introduction

Some people seem to have good fortune all their lives while others appear to face a perpetual battle against adversity. But, however your life turns out, there is one thing you can be sure that you are going to have to deal with, one problem which affects everyone similarly whether they are rich or poor, young or old. At some stage in your life you are going to have to deal with the death of someone you care about.

Isn't it odd that educational systems have been developed which prepare us for almost everything – from baking a cake to sitting an examination, from playing the piano to running a business – and yet at no stage are we taught how to cope with what can be a devastating experience?

In fact, in Britain as in many parts of the Western world, death is something no one likes to talk about. It is only mentioned when there is no way of avoiding doing so and, when someone does have to face the death of a loved one, they will often try to hide their feelings behind a 'stiff upper lip' as though to show any grief would be a sign of weakness.

Death is a fact. It is a natural part of life and the one thing we all have in common. It is only by learning to deal adequately with bereavement and death that we are able to live our own lives to the full.

Because it is not talked about, many people do not understand the complex blend of emotions which accompany bereavement and so, when they find themselves experiencing these emotions, they think there must be something wrong or unnatural about them.

Coming to terms with the death of someone else can often help to reduce the fears associated with thoughts of your own mortality, thus enabling you to go forward to live your life in the most positive way possible. In this book you will find explanations of what is involved when dealing with the loss of someone close and also the best ways of coping positively with the situation both at the time and at later stages in your life.

Note

To avoid the over-use of 'she or he', 'she' and 'he' are used separately, alternately, for the prolonged passages in Chapter 4, but of course children of either gender are being referred to.

CHAPTER 1

About Bereavement

The death of someone close can arouse a multitude of emotions, some of which you would expect and others of which cause you to wonder. Those emotions can vary from extreme sadness to a sense of relief when a life which has been full of pain and suffering comes to an end and the person concerned will suffer no more.

I wonder why so many people are reluctant to allow others to witness how they are feeling – and are in fact embarrassed if anyone should catch them showing signs of extreme emotion. You are a human being, you are allowed to feel grief and sorrow. It is not a sign that you are weak but an indication that you have a warm and caring personality which is affected by the death of another person.

In many cases, particularly if the death was sudden and unexpected, the initial reaction is one of disbelief, even of denial. The mind just cannot take in the fact that the person you love has gone.

Once that initial period of disbelief has passed and you have come to terms with the fact of the death, there are various emotional stages to be experienced before reaching the point of acceptance. The usual pattern of emotional progress after a bereavement is:

Disbelief or denial

Grief

Anger

Guilt

Fear

Acceptance

Peace

Because it is vitally important for your future well-being that you understand and acknowledge the emotions you experience, perhaps we should look at them in turn as some of them may not be what you were expecting.

GRIEF

This is the emotion you would probably expect to feel. But, even though it is common to most situations, there are differences in the depth of grief and in the length of time for which it may persist. After the death of her husband, Prince Albert, Queen Victoria insisted on wearing her widow's weeds for the remainder of her life. Another woman might remarry within a year of her husband's death. Who is to say which is right or which of them loved her husband more?

One might see it as a great compliment to Prince Albert that his widow insisted on demonstrating her grief for the rest of her years. But perhaps it was also a great compliment to the other husband that his widow had found so much love and joy in her marriage that she was ready to repeat the experience quite soon.

Some people are far more able to show their grief openly than others and it is by no means a bad thing to do so. You may not want to walk around the supermarket shedding tears but there is nothing wrong in allowing your friends and family to comfort you when you need it. It is also important, if you have children, to allow them to see this side of you, even though you might feel that you would prefer to spare them the pain it causes.

Sylvia was absolutely devastated when her husband was killed in a car accident on the way home from work. The couple had one child, a four-year-old boy called Mark. Right from the beginning Sylvia decided that she must be strong for Mark and she did her best to explain to the child what had happened in a calm and controlled way. Her motives, of course, were excellent. She thought that Mark would be better able to cope if he felt that his mother was managing to do so – so she kept her tears for the privacy of her bedroom and did her best to remain in control in front of her little boy.

What Sylvia did, however, was cause great confusion in the child's mind. Even at his young age, he knew that crying was associated with being unhappy and, since he never saw his mother cry, he assumed that she was not really terribly unhappy about the death of his father. Naturally he was not able to reason in that way at the age of four, but the memories and feelings were implanted in his subconscious mind at the time, ready to surface at a later date.

And surface they did. Sylvia was amazed when, some years later, Mark accused her of never having loved his father.

If children are to grow up with balanced emotions, they need to know that adults are human beings. We are not perfect people nor are we unfeeling robots. We cry when we are hurt, can be irrational or lose our tempers, can laugh and be happy or even downright silly. All these emotions are part of life and our children need to see us experiencing them and to share them with us.

Grief which is not fully acknowledged and experienced can be physically and emotionally harmful. Everyone has heard of cases where someone has died 'of a broken heart' shortly after the loss of a beloved partner. The heart has not literally broken but the stress caused by keeping grief hidden from the outside world can be enough to affect the blood pressure, heart and will to live of the one left behind.

In my work with the recently bereaved, I am often asked how long this period of grief will last and when it will 'go away'. There is no single answer to this question. Indeed I am not sure that it can ever go away. But it can change and become quite bearable. As the broadcaster David Jacobs once said some time after losing his wife: 'You never get over it but you do get used to it'.

Human beings are remarkably resilient. It has to be that way or no one would ever recover from anything, even tragedies as serious as being in a concentration camp or losing several members of their family at once. No matter how great your grief at the time and no matter how much you feel you will never come through it, you will, *provided you give yourself time to grieve in the first place.*

For most people the first year is the most difficult. There are so many anniversaries to be lived through when you are extremely conscious that someone special is not there. Birthdays, Christmas, Mother's Day, Easter – culminating in the anniversary of the death itself. Survive them once and it will never be as difficult again.

My own husband died in 1982 and for a few years after that I was extremely conscious of the anniversary of the actual date of his death. I would deliberately try to arrange to do something on that day so that I was not alone with too much time to think. But I have to admit that, for the past few years, the date comes and goes without my even being aware of it until some time afterwards.

Time has not altered my sadness at his passing nor the way I felt about him. But life has gone on and there is no reason why that day should really have a greater significance than any other.

It is as well to remember that when we grieve we are really crying for ourselves. It is perfectly all right to do so, of course, but many of us do not stop to realize that this is what we *are* doing. Whatever your personal beliefs about what follows this life (and we will be dealing with that further in the next chapter), you do not need to cry for the person who has died. If there is some special place to go to, then they are there and you should be joyful for them. If there is nothing at all, they cannot be suffering. So accept that you are crying because they have gone and left you behind – perhaps leaving you feeling lonely or frightened. When the crying stops, therefore, it is a sign that you are growing stronger and not that you no longer miss the person who has died.

ANGER

While you will expect to experience grief, you might be more surprised to find that you feel great anger after a bereavement. The reasons for the anger may even vary from day to day. You may find yourself being angry with the person who has died – how dare they go off and leave you behind to cope with everything on your own! Logic may tell you that they had no choice but this does little to reduce the sense of fury at this ultimate 'rejection'.

Another day you might direct your anger towards those who have not suffered as you have. As you walk down the street you will be aware of all those couples who are still together while you have lost your partner. If you have lost a parent or a child, you will notice all those who are not only together but really enjoying each other's company. You may find yourself experiencing not just anger but absolute hatred of all these people – and that can be quite frightening. After all, we are supposed to be civilised human beings who do not hate others – and particularly not for being more fortunate than we feel ourselves to be.

Don't worry. These feelings will soon pass. And, provided you simply acknowledge them without actually doing anything about them, no harm will be done. The victims of your rage will never know what you are feeling and rationality will soon return.

Sometimes the anger is even less logical. You may feel angry because the sun is shining, because the birds are singing or the flowers are beautiful. I remember one young woman telling me she thought she was going mad because 'normal' people don't have such thoughts. But normal people who have been recently bereaved often do. And once you realize that this is just another part of the grieving process, you will be more able to accept that there is nothing wrong with you and this is just another symptom which will soon pass.

GUILT

Guilt often follows a death. It may arise because of unfortunate words spoken in the past which can now never be retracted. Interaction between you and the person who has died may have been bitter and unfriendly – or it may even have ceased altogether – and now there is no way to repair the damage done. If this is the sort of situation in which you find yourself, then the techniques for dealing with the past which will be covered in Chapter 3 will help you.

Occasionally the guilt will have an even deeper basis. Perhaps you were in some way responsible for the death. You may have been driving a car which caused a fatal accident or someone may have died saving your life. Perhaps you had to make the terrible decision to turn off a life support machine.

Let's deal with the last one first. This is something which can never be easy but it is only advised when there really is no hope of recovery for the person concerned. You are being kind not cruel – after all, an existence which depends on pumps, tubes and gauges and where there is no sign of the real person is not a life at all. No one would choose to exist like that. It is probable that, by the time there is nothing left but a mechanically operated body, the spirit has already gone on so you are not really responsible for the death at all.

What such a death does allow you is an opportunity to spend time with the person whose life is ending. Whether or not they understand you on some deeper level, you will have a chance to touch them, to talk to them and to say goodbye.

What about the guilt occasioned because you have accidentally caused the death of another human being? No one can minimize the horror you would feel but death is final and there is nothing you can do about it. There are four main stages to dealing with guilt of this kind:

• Think about your intention at the time. If the event was in fact an accident, you know that you did not intend to hurt anyone. That cannot bring them back to life but it will make it far easier for you to live with yourself.
• Make amends where possible. It may be too late to help the victim but perhaps there is something you can do for her or his family or in her or his name so that some good can come out of a tragic event.
• Learn from the event. Even if you caused a death accidentally, perhaps there is some way in which you can modify your behaviour to try and ensure that such a thing could never happen again.
• Go on with your own life. You may never forget what has happened but the pain will become easier to bear. You will not help yourself, the person who has died or anyone else by dwelling on the subject or allowing it adversely to affect your personality or behaviour for years afterwards.

More often than not, however, the guilt experienced after the death of a loved one is illogical. We tend to dwell on the trivia of life: 'If only I had done this' we think or 'If only I hadn't said that'.

Margot was not very keen on going to the cinema at any time and she found musicals particularly boring. Her mother, however, loved them and when *The Sound of Music* came to the local cinema just before Christmas she asked Margot if she would go with her to see it. Each time the subject was raised, Margot invented another excuse for not going and eventually her mother went with a neighbour to see the film.

A few weeks later the older woman died suddenly and Margot, who had been very fond of her mother, was grief-stricken. After the funeral she found herself becoming extremely depressed; she told me that all she could think of was that she had refused to go to the cinema when it would have been such a small thing to do and would have given her mother so much pleasure.

I explained to Margot that guilt is a natural part of grieving and one that we all have to experience. The fact that she was latching on to such a trivial item only served to prove that she had been a good and loving daughter with no major reason to reproach herself. Her mother knew that she was not fond of musicals and she had not been deprived – she had been to see the film anyway. So Margot could allow herself to let go of the guilt and concentrate on the many good times she and her mother had shared.

FEAR

There is nothing like the death of someone near to us to make us extremely aware of our own mortality. Until you come into contact with death at close hand, dying always seems to be something that happens to other people – and then only when they are very old.

A little bit of healthy fear is not a bad thing if it prevents you driving at a hundred miles an hour down the motorway or developing an addiction to tobacco, alcohol or drugs. But it needs to be kept in proportion. Yes, you are going to die and so am I – that is the only certainty. But we can all choose what we do with the time between now and that occurrence, whenever it may be. We can exist in a state of apprehension or we can live each day in whatever is to us the very best possible way. If all you are going to do is sit around worrying about how the end will come, you might just as well give up now. In fact, some of the people who seem to get the most out of every day are those who know that they do not have much longer to live or those who have had a near-death experience.

One of my patients made a full recovery after a very serious illness which it was not thought she would survive. That woman is now aware of how precious and beautiful each day can be and she tries to do something positive every day of her life. Just like us, she knows that she will die one day but, as she puts it, 'I'm damn well going to *live* until that day comes'.

So accept that it is natural to feel a little more fearful than usual when you have been in close contact with death. But then you must put that fear aside and get on with every single day of your life.

RELIEF

If the person who has died suffered for any length of time, or if it was obvious that they were going to do so, you may well feel a sense of relief when their life has ended. This is not something about which you should feel guilty or ashamed; it is an unselfish thought and shows that you are putting their needs before your own.

If a great deal of the burden of looking after that person has fallen upon your shoulders, you might feel another type of relief too – a release from a physically exhausting and emotionally draining existence. Accept that such a feeling is also natural. You know that, had the person gone on living, you would have continued to do your best for them. What you did is in no way diminished because you are relieved to be released from those tasks after their death.

IMMEDIATELY AFTER A BEREAVEMENT

Once the funeral is over, the family and friends have departed and you realize that life has to go on – but you are not quite sure how – there are various steps you can take.

Look after yourself

Because there is an enormous amount of stress in dealing with a bereavement, you will be quite vulnerable to minor health problems. No one can take the stress out of the situation but you need to do all that you can to prevent that stress from having a harmful effect upon you. So try to establish a healthy routine – even though you may not feel much like it.

Food

You will probably feel disinclined to eat much so, when you do, make sure that what you eat is easy to digest and something you enjoy. If you know that your diet is not well balanced, this is the time to take some vitamin and mineral supplements to make up for it.

Sleep

People tend to react in one of two ways after a bereavement – either they find it extremely difficult to get to sleep at all or else they sleep all the time, as if trying to shut out the realities of the world.

Don't worry if sleep does not come easily in the first few days but, if the problem persists longer than that, ask yourself whether you are doing all you can to help yourself. Use all the old tried and tested methods of inducing sleep – a warm drink, a relaxing bath, a regular routine immediately before bedtime. If sleep still evades you, practise a deep relaxation routine in bed (details of where you can obtain cassettes are under Further Reading). When you are really relaxed, your pulse rate and heartbeat become slower and your blood pressure is lowered – just as happens when you are asleep. If you combine your relaxation with a basic visualization (which can be as simple as imagining a pleasant walk in the country or along the seashore), you will also reduce the mental stress.

Exercise

There is often a tendency, when first bereaved, to sit and do as little as possible. If this is how you feel, allow yourself to do so for the first two or three days but after that try and get yourself moving. You are unlikely to feel like beginning an exercise routine unless this is something you have always done, so the easiest thing is probably to set aside time for a walk, preferably a fairly brisk one, during the day.

Increasing the amount of exercise you take will serve many purposes. On the physical side, it will improve circulation, stimulate the heart and cleanse the body. So long as you do not push yourself beyond whatever your limits may be, you are more likely to return from your walk feeling exhilarated than feeling exhausted. Psychologically this is good for you, plus there is the fact that you will begin to relate to the outside world once more; the longer you spend cocooned in your home, the more difficult it can be to take those first steps outside your own front door.

Keep to a routine

The sooner you can do this the better. There are bound to be days, even some time after the death itself, when you feel miserable or lonely. If, by the time those days come along, you have already re-established a personal routine, it will be easier for you to get yourself going. And just doing things you always do will soon bring you back to a sense of living in the present.

Remember that this must be *your* routine rather than an adaptation of one you have been sharing with the person who has died. And remember too that it does not have to be made up only of tasks which need to be performed – there is nothing wrong in setting aside time for yourself when you can do something for no greater reason than that it brings you pleasure.

Maintain a balance

If you have just lost someone you love, of course you are going to want to think about them. This is not only under-standable – it is right. And if that thinking makes you cry, that is all right too. It would not be healthy to try and force yourself to think of other things all the time and it is quite a good idea to build this 'memory time' into your daily routine. Give yourself a set time each day to sit down and think about the person who has died – but try to do so in a positive way, remembering their good points and happy times spent together. It may help to look through a photo-graph album or listen to a favourite piece of music. In the beginning it may make you weepy but eventually the good memories will overtake the bad ones. And it is far easier to cope with memories you have chosen than to have them take you by surprise during the course of the day.

While memories are good and will remain with you, do not fall into the trap of making your home into a semi-shrine. I have known people – and it is more often women who do this – who have left everything arranged just as if the person who has just died is about to return. To do this is refusing to face reality and is not at all good for you.

Beware of doing as one of my patients did. When her beloved father died, she kept his coat hanging on the stand in the hall and his pipe and tobacco on the table beside his favourite chair. His bedroom looked as if he had just gone out for the day – nothing was allowed to be touched. On the day of her son's wedding, she even went into the room and laid out her father's dinner suit as if he was going to attend the celebration.

No one is suggesting that you go into someone's room the day after their death and clear everything out so that it appears they never existed. Of course you might want to leave some mementoes around – that special gift or an item of particular sentimental value. But it is really important that you accept the truth of the situation as soon as you feel able and strike a balance between acting as though they were about to return and acting as though they had never existed.

Talk

It is good to talk about someone who has recently died if you feel the need – and most people do. Friends and family will probably follow your lead when it comes to how much and how often the subject is raised. They will want to be helpful and supportive but may well be nervous about broaching the subject themselves in case they distress you.

If you feel unable to talk to your friends, you might prefer to contact one of the many organizations designed to help people in your position. Whatever your loss – whether you have been widowed, suffered a bereavement due to a particular disease, have lost a parent, a child or a loved friend – you will find a group of people who have been through the same experience themselves, who therefore understand some of what you are feeling and who truly want to help you. (Addresses of organizations and self-help groups can be found at the end of the book.)

Include happy memories in your talk. Celebrate the life of the person who has gone rather than mourn their death. Many religions have different ways of encouraging just this. After a bereavement friends and family may gather round the bereaved for what appears to be almost a party. Many people nowadays prefer a commemorative service to be a celebration and thanksgiving for the life of the one who has died rather than an occasion for sadness and gloom.

It may be hard to believe in the beginning, but I promise you that the time will come when the spontaneous memories will be of happy times not sad ones – even though you may not notice the change occurring. After my father died some years ago, whenever I thought of him at first the image that came to my mind would be of him looking old and ill. Then one day I realized that I had been thinking about him as he had looked when he was about forty and we used to go for walks together. I don't know when the change in my thinking took place but I do know that the realization of it brought me great comfort and has continued to do so.

REMEMBER...

- It is important to acknowledge and face the emotions you feel when you have lost someone you cared for. These will – and should – include: grief, anger, guilt, fear and relief.
- Look after yourself. Avoid the harmful effects of stress and distress as far as possible by being sensible about your food, sleep, relaxation and exercise.
- Re-establish a routine. Include time to think about the person you have lost but try to think about the happy memories of good times.
- Maintain a balance between acting as though the person who has died never existed and turning your home into a shrine.

- Talk to family and friends or to a self-help group or a professional counsellor.
- Give thanks for the life of the person you have lost instead of brooding on their last days.

CHAPTER 2

What Comes Next?

Many people are so fearful of thinking about death and anything connected with it that they certainly give no thought to what comes afterwards. It is almost as though even thinking about it would hasten the event. This is as foolish as refusing to make a will in case you die all the sooner.

I think it is important for many reasons to stop and consider what you feel happens after death. It may well help to make some future bereavement easier to bear if you believe you know where the person is 'going'. It might also make the thought of your own death some time in the future easier to cope with. And, rather like the will which, once made, can be put in a safe place and hardly ever thought about again, once you have decided upon your own view of what comes next, it becomes as much of an accepted reality as the fact that summer follows spring. You may put this reality away in some far drawer at the back of your mind but, when the time comes for you to take it out and look at it, it will be there, ready and waiting – so much better for you than floundering about unsure of what is happening.

Of course your views and beliefs may change from time to time because of what you see, hear or experience but I think it is beneficial at any time to know where you stand with regard to death and what comes after it. Just as your will may be altered as your financial circumstances change without it actually having been wrong in the first place, so too can your beliefs change as you journey through life, without your earlier ideas being wrong.

For whatever reason, it is not given to us to know and understand precisely what happens after we die – although many people have firmly fixed personal ideas. As you grow and develop you have to find the belief which suits you – one which you feel able to accept and one with which you feel happy. And it is not for me to tell you what that belief should be. With so many wise and good people coming to different conclusions, it is obviously something you have to decide for yourself.

Deciding for yourself is, in my opinion, of more value than blindly following whatever religious precepts were paraded before you as you grew up. Of course it may be that the conclusion you come to is to agree fully with those precepts – and that is fine because you will have thought about it, weighed up the variables and made a conscious decision to agree with those teachings.

When Andrew was at university he had no religious beliefs at all. In fact he would criticize others for their blind acceptance of what was preached to them. He believed that when you died that was it – nothing further happened and there was no lasting sense of awareness, no spirit to be considered. As he grew older and had a family of his own, Andrew found himself becoming increasingly open-minded and willing (or wanting) to accept that there might indeed be some sort of life after this one.

The real change in his outlook came a few years later when, his father having died some time earlier, his mother was in hospital. She'd had major surgery and the doctor told Andrew that it was quite likely she would not survive. For about three weeks it seemed that this was so and Andrew was never at ease, always expecting the dreaded telephone call from the hospital. During the fourth week, however, the old lady seemed to rally. She was sitting in a chair, eating normally and chatting happily with her children and grandchildren. She was so much better that the doctors had decided to send her away for a period of convalescence after which she could return home.

One day Andrew went to visit his mother as usual and he talked to her about the fact that she was going to a convalescent home a couple of days later. Smiling, she shook her head. 'Oh, no', she said. 'I shan't be going anywhere. Your father was here last night and I'll be going with him.' She died peacefully in her sleep the following day.

Whether or not you choose to accept the teachings of a particular religion, there is no doubt that the ritual and ceremony which play a part in the immediate post-death period can be of great help and comfort to the bereaved. There is something reassuring about knowing what you are supposed to do and about following a long-established pattern – whether that means lighting candles, saying prayers, singing songs or acting in any other preordained way. But, of course, you can do this even if you do not follow any particular faith. Bearing in mind that it is the sybolism which is important, you can select your own method of commemorating the life of someone you have lost. One friend of mine always plants a bush if someone he cares for dies; another makes a bequest to her favourite charity. It doesn't matter what you do so long as you know in your heart the reason for the action and so long as it helps you to remember with love the person who has died and enables you to think about them in a positive and joyful way.

There are those who make the supreme gift by allowing organs from the person they have lost to be used to give life to others. One of my patients, Angela, told me how she and her husband had been distraught when their much-loved little girl was killed in a road accident when she was only ten. Nothing could take away their pain and sorrow but the knowledge that her corneas had given sight to two blind people while others had been helped to live normal healthy lives because they received her kidneys and her heart helped them to believe that, painful as it was, there was a purpose to their daughter's death.

It was fortunate that, in this particular case, Angela and her husband had discussed their views on organ donation and had decided that they were in favour of it. Obviously they had been thinking about their own possible deaths when talking about it – no one expects their child to pre-decease them – but having already thought about the subject made it easier and more natural for them to agree when the hospital staff tentatively approached them at the time of their tragedy, than it would have been otherwise.

Whether you feel that you would like your organs, or those of your family, to be used in such a way is, of course, entirely up to you and the people concerned. But, whatever your views, it must be a good thing to talk about it so that you *know* the situation and are not faced with a difficult decision at what is already a distressing time. Like the will, once discussed and decided upon, the whole topic can then be 'put away' until such time as it may be needed.

There are probably as many different ideas about what happens to us after we die as there are people but these ideas tend to fall into three principal categories.

NOTHING THERE

You may choose to believe that this life is all that there is and that nothing at all comes afterwards. When we are dead – that is it!

It then follows that the person who has died cannot be suffering in any way – physically, mentally, emotionally or spiritually – and this could make it easier for the people left behind. Since there is no one alive who has not had pain and problems of some sort, whether great or small, and, since such pain and problems cannot exist if there is nothing at all after death, the person who has died must be better off than they were when alive. Once this concept it accepted, after the initial period of sorrow when we cry for ourselves and what we have lost, there is no longer any need to grieve.

LIFE AFTER DEATH

Even among those who believe firmly that there is a life after death, there are many different ideas of what that life is like. Some people contend that when we die we go to live with God (although different terminology may be used by those from different faiths) or with Jesus. Some feel that there is definitely a heaven and a hell and that we are sent to the one we deserve, there to spend the rest of eternity reaping the positive or negative reward for our earthly thoughts and actions. Yet others believe that there is another world where our souls or spirits go to live.

Whichever belief is yours, it can bring great comfort when you are bereaved. For one thing, it takes away the idea of never seeing or being with the person you loved again. Even if you have years to wait, you will be able to be reunited at some time in the future.

For myself, I am not completely convinced by the concept of a traditional 'heaven' and 'hell' coming after this life. I find the idea of a 'fiery furnace' difficult to accept and I tend to feel that we get our come-uppance for wrongdoings in this life (or perhaps in a future one – but more of that later).

There have been many examples of 'near-death experiences' and of people who have temporarily 'died' – perhaps on an operating table – only to be revived moments later. To my mind, there are too many of these for it to be pure fabrication.

When George was 72 he became very ill and was rushed to hospital where he underwent major surgery. The doctors gently warned his family that he was not expected to survive and, indeed, one night they were summoned to his bedside at the hospital as it was believed that his final hour was near.

There were four elderly men in that ward, one of whom was due to go home just a few days later. This man was a healer attached to the local spiritualist church and, when the family arrived at the hospital, they found him sitting beside George's bed staring at him. His only explanation was that he had woken in the middle of the night with the feeling that George needed him and that he must go to him.

To the amazement of the medical staff, George rallied that night and was well enough to return home about two weeks later. But it was some months afterwards that he told his family of his experience that night.

George had never been a believer in anything of a spiritual nature and certainly had not been able to accept the concept of spiritual healing. He said that, on the night in question, although he was not fully conscious, he knew in his heart that he was going to die. He did not mind this at all, having been so ill that it seemed like a welcome relief, whether or not anything was to come afterwards.

He explained how he had been aware of setting out on a long path towards a distant glow of light and he had known that when he reached the light all would be well. He was halfway along that path when he felt what he could only described as 'someone holding me by the shirt-tails' and this was preventing him from proceeding any further. In the end, the force exerted upon his 'shirt-tails' became so strong that it succeeded in pulling him back and off the path altogether.

Now George had been unconscious throughout the night and naturally his eyes were closed. He had no way of knowing that there was anyone sitting by his bed and certainly not that the man was a healer who was trying to prevent him from dying – even though he did nothing physically to draw him back.

Although he could not really understand what had happened to him, from that night onwards George was aware that there was some force or power great enough to heal. He also became convinced that there was a place to go after death as he *knew* that the path he had been travelling on led somewhere. He had no idea what that 'somewhere' could be like – in fact he did not really want to know. But he told his family that he knew it was a good place because he had felt so happy going towards it and quite resentful at the time that he was being held back.

George lived for about two years after that incident before suffering the heart attack which killed him. I know his widow quite well and she told me that, although naturally distressed when her husband finally died, it made it far easier to bear when she remembered that he was setting out along a path to somewhere he really wanted to go. She also decided that, as the path existed for George, it would also presumably exist for her and that she would see him again when the time came.

Many times a near-death or temporary death experience can dramatically and permanently change the life of the person who has experienced it.

Vanda was in her 30s when she went into hospital for what should have been comparatively minor surgery. There was, however, a severe complication and when she was back in the ward and lying in bed she actually 'died' for about a minute and a half. All her vital signs ceased and the medical staff brought in emergency equipment and were able to revive her.

When Vanda described what had happened some time later, she explained that when she was lying in her bed she was experiencing severe pain. However, once she had 'died', she was totally pain free – was in fact in a warm, comfortable, semi-euphoric state. At the same time she had the experience of rising out of her body and floating somewhere above. Looking down, she could see her body on the bed and could see the nurses and doctors working on her in order to bring her back to life. When they eventually succeeded and she was back in her body, she once again felt the extreme pain she had experienced previously.

A few days later she tried to describe the experience to the doctor who simply shook his head and muttered something about 'lack of oxygen to the brain'. But, as Vanda later pointed out to me, if there was a simple medical explanation for what had happened, how did they explain the fact that she was able to tell them several things which had happened while she was technically dead.

The curtains had been drawn around her hospital bed and and she herself had been unconscious; yet, from her position above her body, Vanda had seen the precise time on the clock high on the wall at the end of the ward and had watched as the lady in the end bed was given a bouquet of yellow flowers which had just been delivered for her. Both these facts she was able to confirm later.

Vanda made a full recovery but her life changed completely. From that moment onwards she decided to explore and investigate what happened after death. She became a spiritualist and went on to become one of the leading mediums in the UK's West Country, giving evidence and bringing comfort to hundreds of bereaved people.

Although we know that no one can prove exactly what happens after we die, Vanda's experiences make very good sense to me and tally with the theories and explanations given to me by other believers. Summarized, we can look on the progress of the spirit in the following way.

When the human being dies, the body being of no further use the spirit leaves it behind. In most cases, rather than progressing immediately to wherever it is due to go, the spirit will remain attached to the earth, often for up to a week or more. This is because it still feels love and concern for those it has left behind and is anxious to see that they are coping reasonably well before it feels able to continue its path. Once the spirit is reassured that, even though still sad, the people who are grieving are managing to pick up the pieces of their lives, it is free to continue its journey of learning and evolvement.

It returns to be near the person or persons left behind whenever it feels that it is needed – perhaps when a particular anniversary brings sadness, perhaps when they need comforting or even to share a moment of joy at a piece of good news.

To me this makes perfect sense. Once you accept that there is another life beyond this one, why should it be that someone who loves you here stops loving you just because you can no longer see them? You don't stop loving them and I am convinced that the feeling is returned.

If you allow it, you may find yourself becoming aware of their presence around you. Some people will just sense that they are near while others have more tangible evidence, often in the form of a scent – a particular perfume or tobacco which was associated with them in lifetime.

Just before my husband's death we were working together on a book which we were writing. He had written books before but for me this was a first time. When he died I decided to continue the work – really as a type of therapy – but of course I had far less experience and expertise than he'd had. I cannot prove what happened to anybody but I know that there were times when I intended to write a certain sentence (and I am a very quick typist) yet, when I looked at the paper, the words which appeared there were totally different. I have to admit that they were always better than my original idea so perhaps this was my husband's way of ensuring that I did our work justice! Whatever the reason, I knew that he was helping me and it gave me great comfort during a difficult period of my life.

Because the person who has died still loves you and still cares about you, don't give up talking to them. Initially you may feel the need to do this quite often but it will probably become less necessary as time goes on.

You can speak the words aloud or you might prefer to think them – they will hear you in either case. If you feel awkward making contact in this way, try talking to a photograph. Somehow, holding their image in your mind and concentrating upon it seems to make contact easier. You will not necessarily get a response – and almost certainly not an immediate one – but they will hear you none the less. So you can continue to share with them the thoughts, joys and problems of everyday life, just as you would have done if they were still with you in the physical sense.

Remember, however, that they still have their own evolvement ahead of them: try not to pull them back too often. If you are still crying out for them or visiting the graveyard on a daily basis some months after their passing, you may well be preventing them from progressing. Show them how deep your love is by letting them go – just as a loving mother has to let her children go however much she wishes they could stay.

REINCARNATION

Some people believe wholeheartedly in the theory of reincarnation while others think that there is nothing at all in it – or even that it is a blasphemous concept. Most people, I would suspect, lie somewhere between these two positions. I work a great deal with past life regression – so it is fairly obvious what I believe. However, I am in no way attempting to convert you to my beliefs; I would simply ask you to be open-minded and consider the possibility.

It would seem to me to be logical that, if we do in fact evolve and progress as we go through an individual life, it is natural for us to evolve even more as we progress through life after life. Just as a child has to complete the syllabus in class 1 before being allowed into class 2, so (I believe) the spirit has a series of lessons to learn in life after life. I do not, however, believe in predestination. As thinking people we come to our own decisions and achieve our own successes or make our own mistakes. If we get it wrong in one life, therefore, the same lessons will confront us in the next one.

Suppose, for example, one spirit elects in a particular

lifetime to learn not to be violent. The opportunity to sub-
scribe to or turn away from violence will be given to the
human being within whom that spirit lives – and it is that
human being who makes the decision about how to
behave and accepts the consequences.

By means of hypnosis, I have been regressing people to
former lives since the early 1980s – and I am by no means
alone as there are several other people who work in this
field. There are so many instances where the person being
regressed has been able to give precise details – names,
dates, places and so on – about which they could not possibly have any knowledge that I believe it is impossible to
say that reincarnation does not exist.

There are other theories, however. Jung believed in an
ancestral memory to which we could all link at times.
Others believe that, time being a purely human concept,
everything is happening *now* and that those who claim to
see into the past or the future are merely more able than
the rest of us to see through the 'clouds' separating the
ages.

I accept the existence of these theories but they do not
take into consideration the spiritual evolvement which I
believe exists. When I have practised past life regression
as part of a course of therapy, there is frequently a definite
progression to be seen from one life to another and this
can often help the patient when it comes to making decisions or overcoming problems which exist in the present.

Although it would be wonderful if we were all to do
everything correctly first time round, it is rather good to
know that, if we should make a mess of it, we can come
back and try again.

Sometimes experiencing a regression to a past life does
not seem to carry us further forward in our personal
evolvement. But perhaps in such cases the purpose of
the experience is to open the mind of the individual to
spiritual possibilities that she or he had not previously
considered.

Dominic was completely honest with me. He was interested in having a past life regression session out of curiosity. He was not sure that he believed in reincarnation but he wanted to find out more. I told him that all I asked was for him to keep an open mind about the topic and not to block what we were doing – and to this he agreed.

At first he was a little disappointed with the previous existence he uncovered. He was an 'ordinary' merchant living an 'ordinary' life in the late eighteenth century. There seemed to be nothing dramatic or meaningful about the facts he uncovered.

During the course of the regression he described to me in great detail a village on the south coast of England where he said he had spent much of his life and where he had in fact died. When we discussed it later, neither he nor I had ever heard of this particular village. Some time later, however, he telephoned me and told me that he had felt the need to travel to the south coast to see if he could find 'his' village. He was at first unsuccessful but, sitting in a local pub one evening he had started a conversation with two elderly locals. Without mentioning the reason for his enquiry, Dominic had asked these men about the village and had been told that its name had been changed some half a century earlier. The following day he travelled to where he now believed it to be and was amazed to find it slightly more built-up than he 'remembered' but very little changed. Later that day he wandered into the local church and discovered a stone plaque in memory of someone of the same surname as he had claimed to have in his previous life. From the dates on the plaque, the person being commemorated would have had to be either his father or some relative of that generation.

So, although that comparatively uninteresting life did not tell Dominic very much about himself, it did convince him that past lives were a reality and thereby changed his thinking – and possibly his future – for all time.

Unlike Dominic, Lorraine's regression was undertaken as part of ongoing therapy for claustrophobia. Now it is quite possible to treat claustrophobia successfully by means of hypnotherapy without ever having to discover the root cause of the problem. But I always offer my patients the choice and Lorraine felt anxious to discover why the phobia had arisen in the first place.

In her past life Lorraine told me that she was a member of a religious order which was struggling to exist at a time of great persecution. When riots took place against the order, Lorraine and the other sisters were captured. They were then given the opportunity of denying their faith, thereby saving their lives, but this was something which they all refused to do.

The punishment for this disobedience was to be walled up alive and this was the fate of the entire sisterhood. Little wonder that Lorraine had carried with her a fear of enclosed spaces.

In this particular instance, because of the strength of faith of the person Lorraine was in that former life, she did not experience particular terror at the time of her death. Her religion gave her a calm and serenity which made it all bearable. But there are, of course, other cases where a life (or a death) has been particularly unpleasant and I would like to reassure you that at no time is the person having the regression allowed to experience any pain – physical, mental or emotional – if they don't want to. There are techniques known to every trained ethical hypnotherapist who practises past life regression which ensure that the patient is able to observe and describe a terrible event without experiencing any more distress than you would now if you told me of the time you grazed your knees as a ten year old. This is why it is important to remember that regression is not a party game and should be practised only by those professionally trained to do it.

You may wonder how it is possible to combine the two beliefs – of life after death and reincarnation. But there does not seem to be any conflict here.

I have found – and here, of course, I can only speak from my experience in the field as I have no way of proving this to you – that it appears to take approximately 70 years from the time a spirit leaves one body until the time it enters another. The exception to this rule is when an individual did not survive for what would have been the normal life span in a particular era. Perhaps there was an early death through illness, injury or accident. In such cases, the spirit returns more quickly as though to 'finish off' what was happening in that lifetime.

So how does this fit in with the concept of life after death in some 'other world'? If you have ever listened to a spiritualist medium giving proof of survival, you will have noticed that almost everyone contacted in the spirit world was of one or two generations back – rarely more. And this is in keeping with the way human beings are. Most of us care very much about those loved ones who are of similar age to ourselves. We also feel extremely strong bonds of love with our children. When it comes to grandchildren, although we love them, the feeling is usually less intense and this applies even more to our great-grandchildren. We might say we love them – and mean it – but they are far more distant from us than our own children were.

So it seems natural that we would want to be around for our partners, our children and possibly our grandchildren. But, by the time it comes to our great-grandchildren, there will be others who are capable of being far closer and more useful to them. After two or three generations, therefore – that is, after about 70 years – the spirit is ready to continue its journey of evolvement and to be born into another body.

Whatever you believe about what happens after death, the conclusion is the same. For the sake of the one who has died, for the sake of those who survive – and, more importantly, for your own sake – there is only one appropriate course of action. Accept that you weep for yourself and that there is nothing wrong with doing so. Then – remembering that you can call upon the one you have lost whenever you feel the need and that you can talk to them at any time – do your best to let them go so that they can get on with whatever is to be the next stage in their evolvement.

CHAPTER 3

Unfinished Business

One of the commonest feelings experienced after the death of someone close is a sense of regret that interaction between the two of you was somehow not quite completed. 'If only...' people say. 'If only I had told him that I loved him...', 'If only we hadn't had a row last time we met...', 'If only I had visited her when I meant to'. All these 'if onlys' – and many others too – add to the guilt, regret or discomfort of the bereaved person.

But life does not consist of neat and tidy compartments. Every situation does not come to a precise and formal conclusion and we human beings are not computerized robots, unable to perform one task until we have fully completed the one before. The lives of many people are so busy that it often is just not possible to fit everything in – and then sometimes we realize we have left it too late.

Even those who have the advantage (from this point of view) of knowing that someone is about to die and therefore that it is essential to speak to them, to make peace with them or to tell them how they feel, often seem to think they can do something about it 'tomorrow'. Only one day they run out of tomorrows.

There are four main categories in this realm of 'unfinished business' and these are:

- things done
- things not done
- things said
- things not said

The various 'things' mentioned may be either positive or negative. One person might regret hasty words spoken in anger while another will feel guilty for not having made some kind comment. One might blame herself or himself for having cheated or lied to the person in the past while another regrets not having been of more practical help. There can be very few people who can look back complacently and tell themselves 'I did and said everything I should'.

Often, however, the act (or failure to act) is far less significant than we think it is. It is just that the bereaved person may need something specific to cling to if she or he is to make any sense of the feelings of guilt, guilt being part of the grieving process.

James had recently started his own business in a small market town in the south of England. This, of course, kept him extremely busy. In addition, he enjoyed spending time with his girlfriend as well as playing squash and swimming with a couple of young men he had known since his college days.

Every few weeks he would travel to Yorkshire where his parents still lived and in between he would telephone them for a weekly chat. During one of these calls, his mother told him that his father had a throat infection and was feeling poorly. She felt that a visit from their son would do her husband the world of good as the two had got on extremely well since James was a child.

James promised to come and see his father as soon as he could but somehow events seemed to overtake him. His financial year came to an end so the books had to be sorted out; his girlfriend's brother got married and they had the wedding to attend; one of his closest friends was to take part in the finals of the local table tennis championship and James had promised to go and cheer him on.

It wasn't that James did not want to go and visit his parents; it was just that he had so many other calls on his time. So he kept putting the trip off, telling his mother each week that he would come as soon as he had a free weekend.

Then one night he received a frantic call from his mother. His father had been rushed into the local hospital after collapsing at home. James did not even stop to pack a bag; he jumped into his car and began the journey north. He arrived at the hospital to be met by his weeping mother who told him that his father had died just minutes earlier.

James was devastated and long after the funeral, was still cursing himself for not having visited his parents earlier. His grief caused him to magnify the enormity of what he had done until he could think of nothing else. By the time he came to see me, he was not eating or sleeping properly and was finding it difficult to concentrate.

I took James through various stages during the course of our counselling sessions. If you have been suffering in the same way after the death of someone close to you – even though the actual circumstances may have been very different – try working through the same stages and it should help you to see things in a more realistic light.

1 LOOK AT THE REALITY OF THE SITUATION

James had not committed a crime. He had not been deliberately cruel to his father. It was not as though he had sat back in front of the television and decided that he did not fancy travelling to Yorkshire – he had genuinely had a great many matters to occupy him during those few weeks. In addition no one had any way of knowing that his father was about to die – all that was thought was that he had a simple throat infection, the type which can usually be cleared up fairly quickly.

2 ASK YOURSELF WHAT THE OTHER PERSON WOULD HAVE THOUGHT

Put yourself for a moment in the shoes of the person who has died. In identical circumstances what would they have thought of your behaviour? Beneath his grief, James knew full well that his father would have understood perfectly. The young man had shown himself to be a loving, caring son who frequently came to visit. He had genuine reasons for finding it difficult to do so at that particular time and those reasons were quite understandable. No reasonable person would have taken offence at them.

3 THINK OF THE GOOD THINGS

Look back at the overall picture of your relationship with the person who has died. Even if, like James, you have some regrets, provided the relationship in general was a good one, you should not waste time reproaching yourself. Better to spend that time remembering happy times together.

4 WHAT GOOD ARE YOU DOING NOW?

Is your sense of remorse actually achieving anything? It cannot be doing you any good if it makes you feel unhappy – or even unwell – and prevents you getting on with your life. Nor can it be of any assistance to the person who has died – whatever your beliefs. If you believe that the spirit of that person is now in some 'other place' (whatever you consider that place to be), surely they will have a greater understanding of human beings and their fallibility than before and will be able to accept any errors and forgive them, in the same way that an adult is understanding when their child is difficult or unruly. It does not make that adult love the child any less and the person for whom you are grieving will feel no less love for you because of some mistake you may have made.

5 APOLOGIZE

It does not matter that the person is no longer around in the material sense. If they exist in a spiritual form they will still hear and understand when you tell them how you feel. So sit quietly and think about them for a few moments and then tell them that you regret how you behaved and that you are sorry. You will find that even if you do no more than this, you will experience a sensation of peace and wholeness once more.

There may be other types of regret which arise after a death. Suppose, for example, there has been ill-feeling or animosity between you and the person concerned. Or perhaps they have been downright unkind or even cruel to you. In such cases there is usually while that person is alive a hope that, eventually, everything will be put right, you will understand how the problems arose and amends will be made. Once they are dead, however, you know this can never be – and that knowledge can be quite devastating however well you may have coped while they were alive.

Ruth was fostered when she was almost two. Her new parents already had two daughters, one of whom had also been adopted and the other of whom was their natural child. The original idea was that after six months of fostering they would apply to adopt Ruth too.

I first met Ruth when she was in her 30s and she told me that for some reason her new 'mother' had never liked her. She did not know why – she could not remember having been particularly bad as a child and she had been quickly and easily accepted by her foster father and the two other little girls.

She had, of course, been very young at the time and her memory was somewhat hazy but she had pieced together

her information from what other people had told her. It appeared that her adoption had been postponed on several occasions and that eventually her foster mother had decided that she did not want her and had returned her to the local authority home when she was just four. There her life had been made a misery by some of the other children who cruelly reminded her that she had not been good enough to be adopted.

Ruth had remained in the home until she grew up. Although she had managed to get a reasonably good job and had made what on the surface appeared to be a satisfactory life for herself, she had never lost the sense of rejection and bewilderment from those early years and had never been able to form close relationships of any sort since that time. All her life she had promised herself that one day she would get in touch with her foster mother and ask her what she had done that had been so terrible and why her foster mother had found it impossible to love her. Although Ruth had discovered the woman's name and address when she was 18, somehow she never got round to doing anything about it – and then she discovered that the woman had died some time earlier, and it was too late.

Ruth was devastated. She told me that she felt a large part of herself had vanished, never to reappear. It left her with a sense of loss she could not quite understand and she did not know how to cope with it. It was affecting her entire life – she was unable to eat or sleep properly and, apart from going to work (where she kept herself very much to herself), she could not face the thought of going out at all or mixing with other people. Her doctor had given her antidepressants and although these had reduced the more obvious symptoms they had done nothing to reduce the sense of anguish she was experiencing.

If you feel that you have been hurt by someone in the past without understanding why, and that person has now died, you might find the following process helpful. (There are also various other techniques given at the end of this chapter.)

1 WHAT FACTS DO YOU KNOW?

If, like Ruth, you were very young, your memory of actual events may be vague or even non-existent. But, even in such cases, there are usually people who can give you the basic information you seek. If you were older, you may well remember a great deal of the situation. If you do, it is possible that distress has made you try to push the knowledge to the back of your mind – but this is not healthy. I do not mean you should spend your life brooding on a past unhappiness but it is necessary to look at it in as much detail as possible just once in order to be able to let it go and store it away somewhere in your mind's vast filing system.

2 DID YOU REALLY DO ANYTHING WRONG?

One of the unfortunate things about someone who has been made a victim is that they often feel that it was all somehow *their* fault. Frequently this is because the person who has been unkind to them has either caused or allowed them to feel this way – perhaps to ease their own conscience.

In cases of child abuse when we can all appreciate that the fault lies with the abuser rather than the child, in the vast majority of cases the abuser will do their best to persuade the child that she or he is (at least in part) to blame.

So now is the time to analyse the situation and ask yourself whether the treatment you received showed a fault in you or one in the person who treated you badly. In Ruth's case, for example, she accepted that she might have been a difficult child, coming as she did from an institutionalized background. But she did not see how she could have been naughty or bad enough to warrant being returned to that institution. She could not understand how any woman – particularly one who was already a mother – could fail to realize the irreparable harm she would be doing to a small child's personality when she rejected her as she did. If she had at least tried to keep channels of communication open, perhaps Ruth would have been able to cope better. As it was, weighing up the whole situation, Ruth decided that the woman was the one at fault and that she herself could not be blamed for what had happened.

3 PEOPLE ARE NOT GOOD JUST BECAUSE THEY ARE DEAD

There is a saying that one 'should not speak ill of the dead'. But a person who was negative or selfish or evil in life does not suddenly become a saint just because they have died. Perhaps it is the thought that they do not have the ability to put their point of view which makes so many people hesitant of criticizing someone who has died. But above all, let's be honest with ourselves and face the fact that the person who has died has their faults too.

There are many types of 'unfinished business' which may exist between those who have died and those who mourn them or are otherwise affected by their death. There are also several different techniques for dealing with this unfinished business so that it is no longer able to affect you in a negative way.

What follow are various examples of these techniques. Naturally it is unlikely that all of them will appeal to any one person. What I would suggest is that you read through them and try the one or two which most appeal to you. You can always attempt the other methods later. Indeed, you may find it best to use a combination of techniques according to your mood and the level of the emotion you are feeling at the time.

None of these techniques are designed to make you forget the past – nor, of course, can they change what has happened. The idea is that you should be able to put the past into perspective, to grieve for the person who has died as much or as little as you find appropriate and then to let them and their influence on your life go on their way, leaving you to live in a happier and more positive fashion.

WRITE A LETTER

If there is something you wish had been said or not said, done or not done, it can be very helpful to sit down and write a letter to the person who has died.

Such a letter can be short or long, depending on how you feel at the time. You do not even have to write it all at once – in fact it is often better to write it over the course of a few days. The most important point of all is to be completely honest in that letter – say whatever is in your heart. You cannot hurt anyone by doing so because that letter will never be sent, the 'recipient' having died. It will, however, be highly therapeutic for you – and sometimes quite surprising – to see your thoughts set down on paper. You don't have to read and re-read the words over a period of years; in fact, once you have written and considered the letter, you may throw it away if you wish.

If you decide to try letter writing, be as spontaneous as possible. Don't worry about formal language or proper turns of phrase – write from the heart. You may find it quite an emotional exercise but better a few tears at this point than misery for years to come.

When James wrote a letter to his father, he began by apologizing for not having come to see him but, by the second page the letter had become a protestation of the love the younger man had for the elder. James then went on to write about the good times they'd had together over the years and how much he felt he had learned from his father. He said he hoped he would be as good a husband and parent as his father had been. So, although writing the first part of the letter made him somewhat tearful, it turned out to be a joyous remembrance of a happy family relationship.

Ruth's letter, by contrast, started quite mildly. She began by asking her late foster mother why she had felt it necessary to send her back to the children's home – 'what did I do that was so bad?' As it went on, however, it became almost vitriolic. Ruth accused the woman of being cruel, selfish and unfeeling and told of her own misery and bitterness at the rejection. 'After all,' she wrote, 'if I had been born to you, you would have kept me and done your best.' The really important part of Ruth's letter was not the anger at the dead woman but the fact that, for the first time, she was able to put into words the hurt and despair she had felt over the years. Having written and re-read the letter she was able to throw it away, and in some way this enabled her to 'throw away' part of her negativity – although she still needed further sessions to help her overcome her difficulty with relationships.

VISUALIZE

If you have something you want to say or questions you want to ask of the person who has died, then visualization can prove to be a highly effective technique. Here is a step-by-step guide to achieving it.

1 First you must relax in whatever way is best for you. There are many different techniques, some of which are available on cassette (*see* Appendix). If you have never practised relaxation before, the simplest method is probably to find a quiet place where you will not be disturbed. Sit or lie comfortably with your head and neck supported and your eyes closed. Starting with your feet and working upwards through your body, tense and then relax each set of muscles in turn – ending with the muscles in your face. Then spend a few moments listening to your own breathing.
2 Now picture the person who has died in as much detail as possible. You are not summoning them in any way,

merely creating a picture in your mind – rather like contemplating an imaginary photograph. Picture them at a
time which was significant to you – whether this is a
time of joy you wish to remember or a time of difficulty.

3 Next, start a conversation with that person. Some people like to do this solely in their imagination while others prefer to speak the words aloud. Do whichever
comes more naturally to you. And, just like the letters
you could write, say whatever you truly want to say. If
you want to express love, grief, regret, understanding or
any other emotion, do so. If you have questions you
need to have answered, ask them.

4 Then remain still and silent and allow the person you
have visualized to answer your questions or say what
they wish to say. You may not necessarily hear them
aloud but you will *know* what it is they are telling you.

You may find it helpful to repeat this process several times
over the course of a few weeks. Because you may feel a little awkward the first time you do it, the response you get
may be minimal. But do persevere and you may learn
things which surprise you – and certainly some which you
find helpful.

There are several explanations for the success of this
technique. Some say that you are really linking with the
spirit of the person who has died and it is that spirit which
is giving you the answer; others that there is nothing there
at all and that your own subconscious mind is furnishing
the answers. Still others believe that there is some memory
within your deep inner mind, including knowledge you
acquired when you may have been too young to understand the words, and that you are dredging up this knowledge from deep within yourself.

I do not know which one is right – or if there is some
completely different explanation. All I can tell you after
years of bereavement counselling is that it is a highly
effective technique. It works. And that is good enough for
me. If it can help someone solve a problem or resolve their

true feelings and thus be able to face the future with increased positivity, I do not feel that I necessarily need to understand the precise mechanics.

MEDITATE

Sometimes there is a longing to be near the person who has died once again – even if just for a short time – to help lessen the pain of the loss and to feel that they are still a part of your life. Bearing in mind the concept that you should not keep a spirit tied to the Earth but allow it to continue its journey and that this method should only be employed on occasions, meditation is a good way of continuing links forged before their death.

Once again you need to begin by finding a peaceful place and relaxing in whatever way you find easiest. People who are new to any form of meditation often find it helps to hold either a photograph of the one who has died or one of their possessions.

For this meditation to be effective, you need to begin by guiding the images which come to your mind. If you were just to sit there and wait for something to happen, all sorts of mundane thoughts would come into your head and block the spontaneous meditation which is to follow.

So start by picturing a room in your own home. See it in as much detail as possible – look at the furniture, the ornaments, the view from the window. Now imagine yourself going to the door of that room and following whatever path is necessary to take you to the front or back door of the building. In your mind, go out of that door and down the path. I cannot describe to you precisely what comes next because every home is different but the idea is to go through gardens, down steps, through gates, whatever is necessary to take you beyond the boundaries of your own home. As you imagine doing this, bear in mind that the person you want to see will be waiting for you at some point.

If you have relaxed sufficiently, the point will come where you will stop thinking consciously of where you are 'going' and some deep inner force in you will take over. You may then find yourself journeying through unfamiliar territory until you come face to face with the person who has died.

The important point when using this technique is to *let it happen*. If you try to force your mind to go in a particular direction, you will put a block on the whole thing and nothing will happen at all.

What takes place when you find the person you are looking for may vary from person to person and even from time to time. Some will have deep and meaningful conversations, others will simply hold hands or embrace. Some may even find themselves being taken somewhere they have never been before.

At some point the image will fade and you will either return to full wakefulness immediately or you may find yourself relaxing deeply for several minutes before opening your eyes.

There are a few points to bear in mind when following this type of meditation technique:

- If it is unfamiliar to you, you may have to practise it several times, or seek the help of a professional hypnotherapist, before achieving anything more than a pleasant relaxation. Please do not feel too disappointed if you do not immediately come into contact with the person you want. It does not mean that you never will. It may be that you are not sufficiently relaxed or it may even be that the spirit is resting and is not yet able to respond.

- You may wonder whether there is real contact being made or whether all this is just a figment of your imagination – something you see because you desperately want to. My own belief is that, because the spirit of the person who has died will always want to protect those left behind, we are allowed glimpses of them and contact with them. But, even if I am wrong and it is just the product of a needy imagination – does it really matter? It is extremely comforting to spend some time, even if only in your mind, with someone you love.

• Interestingly, people who practise this type of meditation often find that in the early days that they visualize the person who has died as they were towards the end of their life. As time goes on, however, that person will almost always be seen as they were when they were closest to the meditator. This will happen spontaneously and you will usually only become aware of it when you realize that they have been looking younger or fitter for some time.

• The first few times you practise this technique you might find yourself feeling physically tired afterwards. Don't let this worry you as it is quite normal for a novice and you will recover within minutes.

MAKE LISTS

There are some people who find the whole concept of visualization or meditation difficult to accept. If this applies to you, try the following.

Make lists of what you and the person who has died gave to each other during their lifetime. I am not talking here about material gifts – although you can make a note of these if you wish. But write about the times you shared, the memories you created, the joys and pleasures you gave each other. Even if there are also some sad times to remember, what did you learn from them? How did you feel about each other – and how did those feelings show themselves?

Your list can be as sparse or as detailed as you wish. After all, it is for your eyes alone and if a word or two serve to bring back a happy memory, why write more? If, however, it gives you pleasure and re-creates the past more vividly to write in some detail, then do so.

Keep those lists somewhere safe so that whenever you feel the need you can read them and feel yourself close once more to the person you love.

FREEZE THE FRAME

This is a helpful way of finishing off whatever unfinished business may remain. It works equally well whether the things to be said or done are positive or negative and it allows the past to be put where it belongs – in the past.

After relaxing, imagine that you are sitting alone in a darkened cinema looking up at the big screen in front of you. On the screen is depicted a scene of particular relevance – one where you feel everything was not said or done. Suppose, for example, you believe now that you should have said some specific words to the person you are thinking of – words which, for one reason or another you did not utter at the time.

When the scene reaches the point where you now think those words should have been spoken, freeze the picture. Now put yourself into the picture and actually speak those words, allowing your imagination to supply the reaction they would have received. Having done that, play the scene through to its end. (You may find it needs to be changed a little from what happened in reality as a result of the new words or deeds you have now included.)

Whether or not you believe that the spirit of the person who has died is aware of what you have done, you will feel the relief of having completed what to you had been unfinished business.

TALK

Speak your thoughts aloud. I truly believe that the person you are speaking to, although no longer 'alive' in the physical sense, will still be able to hear you. Even if you find this difficult to accept, verbalizing in this way can be extremely helpful. Perhaps you will feel that, although you are not making contact with a particular individual, your words can reach God or Spirit (or any other name which to you represents that great and eternal power). At the very least, they will help to keep the person who has died in the forefront of your mind and will lessen the pain of losing them.

CHAPTER 4

The Bereaved Child

Coping with the death of someone you love is a difficult process at any age but particularly so when a child. We have already seen in Chapter 1 how devastating it was for Mark to be shielded from the death of his father – even though his mother was acting from the very best motives and trying to save her little boy from the extremes of grief.

Children experience all the emotions that adults do – often with added complications. Death is an entirely new concept to a small child. The closest she will have come to it is probably in films, in television fiction or on computer games. But that kind of death may be totally divorced from reality (which is why many people believe there should be far greater control – but that is another story). And in such fiction, it is usually only the 'baddies' who die so no one is really unhappy. To lose a loving parent, a kindly grandfather or a baby sister is quite different and children need to be guided carefully and caringly through the entire experience, both when it happens and for some considerable time afterwards.

Of course a child is going to be unhappy when someone they love dies but she is often going to become very frightened too. Suddenly death is real, close at hand and happens to nice people. Her own world is no longer the safe place she thought it was.

A child who loses a parent may become extremely fearful that the other one is going to leave her too. No amount of logical explanation can help; it takes a lot of love and a great deal of reasurance – and no one must ever tell her she is being foolish to think in that way. Some children react by becoming extremely clinging, refusing to let go of the parent who is still alive, afraid to let them out of their sight in case they too disappear, never to return.

Other children will react in a totally different fashion and will become extremely offhand with the surviving parent, possibly refusing even to hold their hand or kiss them goodnight. A child who acts in this way is sub-consciously preparing herself for the loss of this second parent – as though saying 'Look how well I can cope without you'.

Both these forms of behaviour are cries for help and understanding. So – bearing in mind the limitations imposed by age and comprehension – the more you are able to tell your child the truth, the better. It may be dis-tressing to know that daddy died from a particular illness or that mummy was knocked down by a car but it does reinforce the fact that the parent did not choose to leave and that she or he died in a way which does not affect most people so the chance of it happening to the surviving one is remote.

If the death was that of someone of her own age – and especially from her own family – that may create enor-mous fear in the mind of the child. The questions which will flood into her mind – but which she may never state aloud – will include, 'Am I going to die too?' and 'Do they wish it had been me?'

All at once she realizes that death does not only happen to baddies or even to old people. It happens to children too. Suddenly she is made aware of her own mortality – and that can be very scary. She does not want to die, she does not want to suffer. But she does not know how to prevent it.

If it was an illness which caused the death of the young person, the child remaining may well develop psychoso-matic symptoms of the same or a similar condition. Her already-present fear will then have something positive to feed on.

Alan's younger brother had suffered from a heart condition since birth and their parents had known all along that it was unlikely that their younger son would survive. Alan had been three years old when his brother, Joe, was born. Until that time he had been a normal, noisy, mischievous toddler but, after the arrival of the baby, things had changed. Now he wasn't allowed to shout and bang doors as he had previously in case it disturbed the baby.

Until that time, as an only child, Alan had received a great deal of attention from both his mother and father but once Joe was on the scene that attention dropped. Of course the birth of any younger child would be likely to take up a fair amount of the parents' time, but Joe had special needs and so both mother and father spent a great deal of time looking after him. It would not have been unnatural for Alan to be jealous, even had Joe been a normal healthy baby, but in this case the situation was made even worse. Because of Joe's weakness, Alan was not able play his part in caring for his brother. No one asked if he would like to hold the baby; he had to be quiet so that he did not wake him; his mother was always too tired and his father too busy to read him his usual bedtime story. Little wonder that Alan decided he did not like this baby much. But he knew his parents obviously did – they were always touching or stroking the baby. Alan began to feel that they far preferred Joe to him.

Then, when Alan was nearly six, Joe died. Naturally both parents were extremely distressed and spent much of the early period crying and talking about their younger son. So much so that Alan began to wonder whether they were crying because Joe had died and he was still there.

Of course this was not true. Alan was loved by both parents. It was just that Joe had taken up so much of their time and energy that they had less to spend on their other son. They had not dreamed for a moment what was going on in Alan's head and were quite unprepared for his difficult behaviour after Joe died.

I met Alan when he was in his 20s and although his logic now told him that his parents had loved him and he now understood the reasons for his brother's early death he could remember clearly thinking that he would *make* his mother and father pay attention to him and, if the only way to do that was to be naughty so that they shouted at him or smacked him, that would do.

Because children find it so difficult to put their feelings into words, it is very easy for adults to misunderstand what is going on in their minds. So it is really important to let a child share in whatever is going on as much as possible and to talk to them about what is happening – even if they do not yet fully understand what you are saying.

GUILT

We have seen how one of the natural emotions to follow a bereavement is a sense of guilt. Nowhere is this more true than in the case of a child.

Children often feel guilty when someone dies because they think it was because they were 'naughty' or 'not nice enough'. They see the death as a personal punishment. It is vitally important to reassure a child at such a time that he is in no way responsible for the death and that it would have happened whatever his behaviour.

Enormous damage can be done to the child's future self-image if care is not taken at this time. Because children naturally tend to think of adults close to them as wise and wonderful creatures who can do no wrong, should one of those wonderful people leave, it must mean that they (the child) were not sufficiently lovable to make them want to stay. Whatever the facts, a child will often take the loss of someone close as a deliberate rejection and this will lead them to form an image of themselves as someone who is unworthy, unlovable and who deserves to be rejected. If not noticed and handled in the appropriate way, these feelings can cause them to grow up into the type of people who enter one disastrous relationship after another as they seek subconsciously to perpetuate the self-image which was formed at the time of that early tragedy.

Another cause of guilt in a child is when they find themselves laughing and being happy again – perhaps not too long after the death. A child needs to be reassured that life does go on and that by allowing ourselves to enjoy that life we are not showing that we loved any less the person who has died.

UNFORTUNATE WORDS

Particularly if you are dealing with very young children, it is advisable to be careful of the words and phrases you use. Because children can be so matter-of-fact, it is probably better to use the term 'died' than some phrase such as 'gone to sleep', 'gone to Heaven', 'gone to be with Jesus'. Such terminology can set up a problem of its own in the mind of the child.

When Beverley was five her grandmother died. Because she had lived about a hundred and fifty miles away, Beverley had not seen her all that often so, although she was sad and she saw that it made her mother sad, she had not found the death too difficult to cope with. Her mother wanted to explain the concept in terms that the child would understand and had told her that 'Granny has died and gone to live with God and Jesus'. This Beverley unquestioningly accepted.

The family was not a particularly religious one but they would go to church on special occasions – such as Easter, Harvest Festival and Christmas. The little girl usually accompanied her parents on such visits. However, when the time came for the family to attend the carol service in the church, Beverley became quite distressed, crying and hanging on to her mother while begging her not to go.

To Beverley, the church was a place where God and Jesus lived and because of the explanations after the death of her grandmother, Beverley had come to believe that this was where the old lady had gone. She developed two great fears. One was that the church would be full of dead people and the other was that anyone who went there would never come back again. She was terrified that if her mother went to church she would die and they would never see each other again.

A woman of my acquaintance told me that she had seen her uncle in his coffin when she was just a child. He had his eyes closed, just as if he was asleep. For some time afterwards she had tried desperately to stay awake all night, fearing that if she closed her eyes she would die and never be able to open them again.

SHARING

Talking to your children and allowing them to share the emotion of the moment is essential if they are to grow up with a strong self-image and the ability to cope with death in the future.

Let your child see your feelings. If you are unhappy and need to cry, let them know it. It will probably make them cry too but this is no bad thing. Children need to know from a very early age that emotions exist and should be acknowledged. This will help them throughout life to become more aware and understanding of other people's feelings, hence more caring and compassionate people.

Don't just talk to them about the death itself but, as time passes, talk about the person who has died. Tell them stories of good times shared and make such comments as 'Daddy would have liked that' or 'That was Granny's favourite colour'. In this way you will be able to instil in them a sense of continuity and of being able to love, and be loved by, someone they can no longer see.

If you have photographs around the house showing the person who has died, leave them there. As the child grows up, he will be able to look at them and know who they were and will be encouraged to talk about them. But, as discussed in Chapter 1, don't be tempted to turn your home into a 'shrine'. It is natural to keep photographs or mementoes around you – but not to leave the house looking as though the dead person is about to return at any moment. Leaving the coat on the hook and the shoes in the hall will cause considerable confusion for a child who is trying desperately to come to terms with the fact that the person who has died will not be coming back again.

People react differently after a bereavement. Some will visit a cemetery frequently, to tend the grave and lay flowers; some will go only on special occasions – birthdays or Mother's Day, for example; while others will not feel the need to go at all. Whatever you decide, give your child the opportunity to join you but don't compel them to do so. And bear in mind that a graveyard need not be an unhappy place and therefore going there does not have to be an unhappy occasion. Let it be far more a celebration of the love felt for the person who has died than grief at their passing. In the early days after the death there may naturally be tears and sadness. But, as time goes on, let it be a time of peace, love and respect.

One friend of mine, whose mother died when she was just ten, told me that, as a teenager, she would go and sit on the grass beside her mother's grave and talk to her just as though she were alive. She would tell her about what was going on in her life, her hopes and her fears and although she knew she could never get a reply in the ordinary sense she always came away feeling peaceful. She had a loving father and two younger brothers but only this communion with her mother could fill a particular void in her young life.

Just as it can be comforting for an adult to talk to the person who has died, it can be even more so for a child. It helps them to accept that there is a continuity in life and in death and to feel less abandoned and alone. So it can be helpful to discuss with your child the possibility of talking to the person they have lost. Naturally you need to explain that they will not receive an answer in the way which is usual to them but they also need to know that this does not mean that their words will not be heard.

Do be careful, however, to avoid the concept of the 'all-seeing eyes'. Toby was only six when his father died. After the initial grieving period, his mother explained to him that, although his daddy could not be there with him any more, he still loved him, was still looking after him and still wanted to know what was going on in his life. She told the little boy that he could talk to his father at any time and that his words would be heard because 'daddy is everywhere that you are'.

Toby accepted this idea quite happily but, over the next couple of weeks, he became more and more withdrawn. Eventually it turned out that he thought his father was watching him whatever he was doing and, not wanting to let him down by doing anything naughty, he had been scared to do anything at all. Fortunately in Toby's case this was noticed very quickly but it is not uncommon for a young child to react in this way.

RITUAL

Children respond very well to ritual. After all, their lives are made up of doing pretty much the same things at the same time every day – and think of all those nursery rhymes with their set actions. They will also respond well to the ritual which accompanies a death as it will help them to come to terms with what has happened and to accept it as part of life.

This ritual may or may not be linked to religion – depending upon your beliefs and what you choose to do. But, whether you light a candle, say a prayer, give a donation to charity or plant a bush in the garden, allow your child to play his part in the proceedings.

CHILDREN AND PETS

Remember that to a child the death of a beloved pet – be it a dog or a mouse – can be just as distressing as the death of a human. When a child gives love, it is given unconditionally and so the same love is given to a small creature as to a person.

Because of this, the child needs to be allowed to go through the entire grieving process with all that it entails and should never be made to feel that the creature he is mourning is not worthy of all this emotion.

In some ways, sad though it is, the death of a pet can help a child understand the concept of life and death. In most cases the life span of a small animal is less than that of a human, so it means that the child is going to have to learn at some point how to deal with a bereavement. It can often be seen that children brought up on a farm are able to cope far better with death throughout their lives because they have been so used to observing it from an early age.

Should it become necessary to have a pet's life ended by the vet due to its poor health, then, harrowing as it may seem at the time, it is only fair to tell the child in advance – provided, of course, he is old enough to understand what you are saying. Even though it will be a time of tears and sorrow, it is right for the child to have the opportunity to say goodbye to a loved friend if at all possible. You might feel that it would be kinder to say nothing and quietly have the deed done – but can you imagine the heartbreak of a child coming home to find his beloved pet has gone, never to return, and never having had the chance to touch it for that last time. Quite apart from the grief it will cause the child, it could well damage his faith in you if he ever learned that you had known in advance what was going to happen and had not told him.

Although most people – adult and child – who have loved one animal will go on to have another, in the case of a child this must be done when he himself is ready. If he has truly loved his pet and that pet has just died, simply to go and out get another must seem as horrifying to the child as it would be to a bereaved mother to be told that she can always have more children. No baby can replace one which has died and no pet can replace one which has died, so allow time for the child to grieve and then see if he is ready to look after and love another animal.

REMEMBER…

- Your child will be experiencing emotions which are similar to your own but she will not yet have the ability to understand those emotions. It is important to talk to her about your shared loss and grief so that she realizes she is understood. Use words and phrases which are appropriate to the age and understanding of the child concerned.
- Let the child take part in the official mourning, however that is conducted. Whatever your religion – or if you have none at all – children benefit greatly from the use of ritual at such times. It may be the ritual laid down by the elders of a particular faith or it may be the simple act of placing a flower in a special place to commemorate the person who has died. Whichever it is, it will help the child to acknowledge the loss and come to terms with it.
- Make sure your child realizes that the death is not some kind of divine retribution for bad thoughts or behaviour and that she is in no way responsible for it. Nor has she been in any way rejected by the person who has died.
- Don't send a child away unless it is absolutely essential. If, for some reason, it *is* essential, explain what is happening and promise to have your own private 'ceremony' when she returns. Never try to pretend that the death hasn't happened or that it isn't going to affect her life – because it is.
- A child should be allowed to go through all the phases of grief, just as an adult should. She will experience sor-

row, anger, fear, loneliness, anger, lack of understanding and guilt. As you already know, this is quite normal but she herself is unlikely to realize this and may need to be encouraged to talk about how she is feeling so that she can be reassured.

- Share your own emotions with your child. Let her cry as much as she needs and let her see you cry too. Allow her to talk as it is only in this way that you will understand what she is thinking and feeling. Let her ask you questions and do your best to answer them as honestly as possible, taking into consideration her age and ability to understand.

- Talk to the child about death in general. Make sure that she realizes it isn't the inevitable result of every illness or every accident or she may become fearful of life in general and particularly of hospitals, the police and so on.

- Talk about the person who has died in as natural a way as possible. Let the child know that the one they have lost is still near and still loves them. Suggest that she might like to speak to them but don't allow her to think she is being watched at every moment.

- Provided she is old enough to understand what is going on (usually from about four years old upwards), allow the child to be present at any later ceremony or service which may be held. Tell her in advance what to expect when she gets there.

- You are not trying to pretend that the person who has died never existed, so don't immediately remove all evidence of them from your home or your conversation. However, avoid turning the house into some sort of 'shrine' to their memory – and in particular, avoid making it look as though they could return at any moment as this could be extremely frightening to a child.

- Take care with the words you use. Try and avoid such phrases as 'having a long sleep' as this can cause unfortunate links in the child's mind and might make her fearful of going to sleep herself. If you wish to use such phrases as being 'with God' or 'with Jesus' make sure the child knows the difference between this concept and going into a church.

- Children – like adults – should be allowed to remember and commemorate aniversaries and special days. However, this should not be done in a morbid or sorrowful way but rather as a celebration of the life of the person who has died.
- Sometimes a child will feel the need to see the scene of death. If this desire is expressed, and if it is at all possible, she should be allowed to.
- If your child wants to go the cemetery he should be allowed to do so – but try to help him see it as an opportunity for remembering the good things about the person who has died rather than as a time for grief. If he is unwilling to go there never force the issue as this could create problems later in life. Older children may feel the need to go there alone, particularly if it is a parent who has died, and their need for this private communion should be respected.
- If it is his brother or sister who has died, don't cut the child out. Let him share your grief and take care to reassure him that he is still loved for himself. Keep a look out for the onset of psychosomatic illness and take care never to say anything to make him think you wish he had gone instead.
- Because many children experience a sense of guilt when they find themselves laughing and being happy again, they may need reassurance that there is nothing wrong in this and that they – and you – can be getting on with life and enjoying it as this does not imply that the person who has died is not being missed.
- Children really love their pets so allow your child to grieve for his animal in the same way as for a person. If it is possible and appropriate, give him time to say goodbye to his pet. If you decide to give him another one, wait until he is ready and then try not to imply that this is a replacement for the one who has died.

CHAPTER 5

The Loss of a Child

There is probably no bereavement harder to deal with than the loss of a child. Even though we all know it can happen – and, indeed, most of us know someone to whom it *has* happened – we never expect our children to die before us. And there is no loss more likely to create a sense of guilt within the parents – even when there is nothing with which they could possibly reproach themselves. There is always the thought of: 'Should I have done something differently?' 'Ought I to have noticed what was happening?' or simply 'Was it my fault?'

Claudia and Eric were told when their little daughter Jessica was very young that she had an incurable form of leukaemia and that she would probably only survive for a few years. Knowing this, they determined to give her as normal and happy a life as possible. This they did, allowing her to play outside with other children and her little brother Jamie. Naturally they did their best to keep her healthy and she was given all necessary medication but they decided not to let her think of herself as an invalid or as someone who was 'different' from the other children in the street.

To an outsider Jessica looked the picture of health – she was a pretty, blue-eyed, blonde child with laughing eyes and bouncing curls. But she had only to catch a cold and she would become desperately and dangerously ill.

Three days after her sixth birthday, Jessica died. The end when it came was sudden – she had only been ill for a matter of hours. I spoke to Claudia about a week afterwards and she told me that although they knew just what was wrong with their daughter somehow they never really expected it to happen. When she was poorly, they would obviously be extremely concerned. But she always seemed to rally and, when she was well, they would feel that she would go on like this for ever. So the shock to parents who have been given warning of their child's imminent death can be as great as that experienced by those to whom the death is completely unexpected.

At first Claudia and Eric tormented themselves with the thought that had they compelled Jessica to lead a more cushioned and protected life she might not have died so soon but after the initial period of grief and self-recrimination they decided that they had done the right thing. Jessie had six joyful years as a happy, friendly, laughing child who enjoyed all the good times and, because of that, was able to cope soundly with the bad times. Her parents came to the conclusion that this must be better than having a small daughter who may have lived an extra year or two but who had been forced to spend all her time being cosseted and watching life through a window.

If you (or someone you know) has the misfortune to suffer the death of a child, you will probably be bombarded with all sorts of guilty feelings immediately afterwards. But ask yourself whether what you did was what you thought was best for the child at the time. If you can answer this honestly in the affirmative, you have nothing with which to reproach yourself.

If we go back to the concept of spiritual progression through a series of lives, with the spirit entering a human body in order to learn its chosen lessons, surely those short lives must have been chosen by a spirit with little more to learn. I truly believe that it is a great privilege to have had our lives touched, for however short a time, by spirits so evolved that they didn't have to stay here for long. I also think that sometimes the spirit is so evolved that it has nothing further to learn for itself but merely came to the earth in order to teach us something.

And if you accept the principle of life after death you do not lose your child for ever. There will be a time – however far in the future – when you will be reunited in a place where nothing more can hurt either of you. Spiritualists believe that children continue to grow in the life after this one – and this appears to have been borne out by the experience of a friend of mine.

This woman (I'll call her Mary) has three healthy teenage children. But, many years ago, before any of her present children were born, she had to cope with the premature birth and almost instant death of two baby girls. More recently, Mary's father died and she took her mother to the local spiritualist church in the hope that she would derive some comfort from the medium who was speaking there. And indeed this medium did give evidence to Mary and her mother of her father's continued spiritual existence. Just before she finished speaking, she turned to Mary and said: 'Your father says you are not to worry – he's with the girls.'

Mary was confused. What girls? It was some hours before she realized that it must mean the two children she had lost. But she had never thought of them as 'girls' – to her they were always 'babies'. But, thinking about it now, how natural it seemed that they should be with their grandfather and how comforting to think that they were all together.

Most people find it difficult enough to find the right words after any sort of bereavement but when you lose a child other people never seem to know what to say. Often they think it best to avoid the grieving parents altogether and although their motives may be right this is definitely the wrong thing to do. Anyone who has suffered a loss needs to be able to talk about it and a true friend will be willing to sit and listen, comforting where possible or just providing a hand to hold and a shoulder to cry on if that is what is needed at the time.

Those who seem to find it the most difficult to talk to a newly bereaved parent are often other parents. One such woman told me that she felt embarrassed about going to visit a neighbour whose child had recently died because she had two fit and healthy children of her own. She did not know quite what she expected – whether the grieving mother would resent her because her children were still alive or whether this would make her unable to bear the sight of her. So awkward did she feel about this that she started taking her children to school by a different route so that they would not have to pass the bereaved mother's house.

Life will never be the same for someone who has lost a child but once the immediate grieving period is over it has to return to some semblance of normality. And normality includes people of all generations from the very young to the very old. Bereaved parents need to find their way back to this 'normal' life just as much as anyone else. So do go and visit them and talk to them. You may not wish to take your children with you initially but there is no necessity to hide them from view.

Each individual will require a different amount of 'acute grieving time' before being ready to face the world again. So the kindest thing to do is to issue any invitations while explaining that you quite understand if they do not feel ready to accept them yet. The first time they do venture out into the world again, offer to accompany them so that they do not fear either being avoided because other people feel awkward or being overwhelmed by declarations of well-meant sympathy with which they might be unable to cope.

You will also need to follow their lead when talking to them. Sometimes they might feel a great desire to talk about the child they have lost while at others it might be too painful and distressing to do so. Be ready to adapt your own conversation according to their wants – and don't feel embarrassed if they ask you questions about your own children; it could be that they need to be reassured of the continuity of the world beyond their own grief.

MISCARRIAGE

While everyone can sympathize with those who have lost a child and even with those who have suffered a stillbirth, many people still find it difficult to think of a miscarriage as a bereavement. But that is just what it is. Even if the mother has only been carrying that new life for a few short weeks, it is still her child and the loss of it can cause her enormous grief.

I have worked extensively over the past two years with many women who have suffered a miscarriage – and some who have experienced more than one. Looking through my files, I find the same feelings coming up time and time again:

- Guilt. The woman is often tormented by wondering whether she did something foolish which caused the miscarriage to occur.
- Fear. Will it happen if she becomes pregnant again? Suppose she can never have a child.
- Why me? The woman looks around at all those other women who have children – sometimes more than they planned for – and wonders why she should be the one to be different. And yet statistics show that early miscarriage is actually very common. In *The Well Woman's Self Help Directory* (published by Sidgwick and Jackson, 1990), Nikki Bradford writes:

Miscarriage is thought to be the single most common complication in pregnancy and is the reason that brings young women into hospital most often. Very early miscarriages may affect up to one in two pregnancies.

- No one understands. I have been amazed at the lack of understanding shown to women who have had miscarriages. One young woman's doctor told her to 'look on it as a heavy period' while another was told 'oh well, you're young – you can always try again'. Well-intentioned possibly but totally ignoring the fact that their unborn babies had just died.

- Sense of isolation. However much partners care and however grief-stricken they may feel at the loss of their unborn child, they are not in the same position as the women themselves because they have not been carrying that baby inside them. One of my patients said that she felt like screaming every time her husband said 'I know how you feel'. He was a lovely man who was truly distressed at the loss of the baby but, as his wife, said 'he has never felt it move inside him – he *cannot* know how I feel!'

- There is nothing to show that the baby ever existed. This is one of the hardest things for many women to bear. Everyone else has something – from a matinée jacket to a photograph – to acknowledge the existence of the child they have lost. The mother who has miscarried has nothing. I usually suggest to my patients that they go out and buy something to mark the life of their unborn child. It does not matter what it is – one woman had a glass goblet engraved while another bought a teddy bear. Those who are religious might choose something appropriate to their faith while others might buy a plant to put in the garden. (A word of warning here – while I think it is an excellent idea to commemorate a life with another living thing, do be sure to choose a fail-safe plant like a rose or a shrub. At this vulnerable time there would seem to be a terrible significance if you choose a more fragile plant which does not thrive.)

- No one talks to me. One young teacher who was away from work for a while having suffered two miscarriages in the course of a year was devastated to find that she heard nothing from any of her colleagues. This was probably due to embarrassment on their part at not knowing what to say – but that does not excuse their insensitivity. When she did bump into one of them in the supermarket, the woman simply asked her 'are you better now?' – as if she had been suffering from a cold or flu.

It is important for anyone who has suffered a miscarriage for which there is no known explanation to give herself time before attempting to become pregnant again. There is a great temptation to fill the emotional void by having a baby as soon as possible but, apart from the fact that hormonal balance will need to be achieved if a future pregnancy is to be successful, mental and emotional stability are important too.

Because a miscarriage can seriously affect a woman's confidence about future pregnancies, take the time to ensure that you are as physically and emotionally fit as possible. There is an excellent organisation called Foresight (details in *Useful Addresses*) which specializes in promoting preconceptual care for both mother and father, thus ensuring that both parents are in the optimum physical and emotional state before the baby is even conceived.

STILLBIRTH

The death of a baby becomes a stillbirth after the 24th week. Because the child within her will by then have been growing and moving for quite some time, the mother will have been thinking of it far more as if it had already been born. Perhaps a room has been prepared as a nursery; she may have acquired a collection of tiny clothes wrapped in tissue paper; a name may even have been chosen for the baby. The loss at this stage is naturally devastating to both parents but particularly to the mother who is the one who has been carrying the child within her.

Many hospitals now allow a photograph to be taken of a fully formed child who did not survive. I have known several mothers who have had this done and, even though it was too painful actually to look at that photograph for some time, they have all been pleased at a later date to have in their possession a physical memento of their lost child. So, whatever you feel like at the time, if this facility is offered to you, it might be helpful in the long term to take advantage of it.

It is also helpful to go ahead and name the baby, even though you were never able to take her or him home with you. Anything which can be done to acknowledge the child's existence will bring you comfort once you have dealt with the immediate trauma of the situation. At this stage too, of course, it is possible if you wish it to arrange for a funeral and a service and many people derive comfort from doing so.

If other people find it difficult to know how to approach a woman who has suffered a miscarriage, the situation is even worse when there has been a stillbirth. Unfortunately, there are no 'appropriate' words at such a time and people are often frightened of opening a floodgate of tears which they will be unable to stop. But please, please, if you know of anyone in this situation, the one thing they need is to have their friends and family around them. If you can't think of anything to say, tell them so. Put your arms around them, give them a hug and let them know you are there. That is all you can do. No one can take away the pain they are suffering but at least you can let them know they are not suffering in isolation.

If you have had such a tragedy in your life, do try and find the opportunity to talk about it. If you really feel unable to talk to those who should be closest to you, then find a professional to help you. A properly trained and qualified counsellor will be able to support you through the hardest times and help you – when you are ready – to plan for the future.

COT DEATH

There must be little that is more devastating than walking into the room where you laid your happy, healthy baby down to sleep only to find that same baby has died for no immediately apparent reason. Although statistics show that the number of cot deaths is falling, this still happens to far too many parents each year.

Apart from the obvious tragedy of losing their child, the parents then have to wonder whether it was something they did or did not do which caused (or contributed to) that death. Suppose they had laid the baby down in a different position...what if the bedding had been made of different material...why didn't they come into the room ten minutes earlier? All these questions and many more run through their heads at such a dreadful time.

But there are no answers. Even experts will give you conflicting responses to these questions. There are many theories put forward and suggestions made but no one is absolutely sure why cot deaths occur. That being the case, you should not reproach yourself. You did all that you possibly could to look after the child you loved, but for whatever reason that child was not meant to survive and grow – or not in this world anyway.

At a time like this, once the immediate trauma has subsided, the parents will be greatly in need of company and support. Apart from the extreme grief they are suffering, they need to see that there is no accusation or blame in the eyes of their friends if they are to rid themselves of any sense of responsibility for the tragedy.

One of the effects of experiencing a cot death is that the parents are likely to become over-anxious about any other children they have or may have in the future. I have known women who, after the birth of another child, absolutely refused to go anywhere, day or evening, unless the child was with them. One mother placed her next baby's cot beside her bed and then woke every half an hour or so during the night and checked that the child was still breathing. While this is fully understandable, it is not good for either mother or child.

The only thing to do is naturally to take every care and precaution for the baby's safety and then treat them as normally as possible. Smothering your child with attention will be exhausing and stressful for you and stifling for her or his personality.

ILLNESS

Some children are born with a life-threatening disease or – like little Jessica – develop it in early childhood. Others lose their life after a comparatively short period of illness. In either case they leave a gap in the life of their parents and family which causes great pain and distress.

If your child has a chronic condition which you know is likely to be responsible for cutting their life short, you have one very important decision to make. Do you do everything you can – within the constraints of that condition – to allow your child to live as full and active a life as possible, even if it means that that life is a little shorter than it might otherwise have been? Or do you protect your child as much as possible from the outside world, thereby extending the quantity, if not the quality, of their life? It would be impertinent of me to try and make that decision for you; different aspects will have to be taken into account in each individual case and a great deal of thought – and sensible advice – will have to go into the decision. But I would urge you to consider making that decision and then follow it through as far as possible. It will go a long way towards avoiding the 'if only' which so often torments bereaved parents.

Remember, too, if you have lost your child after an illness – whether or not it went on for a long time – your own physical and emotional health is likely to have suffered too. There may well have been sleepless nights or hard physical work involved in caring for your child – and although of course you did it willingly and lovingly, nonetheless it will have taken its toll on your physical wellbeing. In addition you have suffered the torments of knowing what was likely to happen and the stress this causes can also affect your health. Most people are able to cope reasonably well while the situation continues but as soon as it is over all the accumulation of physical, mental and emotional tension manifests itself in some form.

Although you may find it hard to think of yourself when your child has just died, it is vital that you take care of yourself now. Sleep may not come easily at first to some – although others find that they want to sleep (to shut out the realities) all the time – but you can practise a relaxation technique which will have a regenerating effect on mind or body. You may not feel like eating – but there are available excellent sources of essential vitamins and minerals.

If you have other children, if you hope to have any in the future – or if you do not want to betray the love of the child you have just lost – you owe it to yourself to look after your health.

Those of us who believe in a life after this one also believe that in that world (whatever it may be like) we are made whole again. Wherever your child has gone, there is no pain, no suffering, no fear. One mother whose ten-year-old son died from cancer three years after having a leg amputated because of the disease told me that she used to dream of him regularly. At first she would picture him as he had been in the last year of his life but gradually he appeared to grow healthier and one day she actually saw him running through a field on two good legs. A grieving mother's fanciful imaginings? I don't think so. If there is a place for us to go where there is peace and wisdom, it makes sense to me that we would all be healed sufficiently to benefit from it.

Even if you believe that there is nothing at all after death, you must accept that your child is no longer suffering. So cry by all means – but remember that you are crying for yourself and your loss. Whatever your beliefs, your child is not hurting now.

ACCIDENT

By definition, an accident is a sudden occurrence – and because of this the shock to the system is increased. If death follows, it may be immediate or it may be after a protracted period of suffering and anxiety. The stress experienced by the bereaved is therefore heightened; one moment your child is there, fit and strong, and the next moment she or he has gone. Is it any wonder that the guilt of the bereaved at such times is enormous? 'If only we hadn't let her cross the road alone...' 'Why didn't he come straight home...' 'I should never have let him go on that outing...'

I have told you of my beliefs about the progress of the spirit from one life to another as part of an evolvement process. Although I do not believe in predestination in all things, I do think that the one thing that spirit has decided before it even touches this life is the moment of death of the person concerned – not necessarily the method of that death, but certainly the time at which it is to take place.

You only have to look at the number of people who – seemingly by chance – were in the right or the wrong place at the time of some disaster to see that it appears to have been ordained that some should die while others should live. There was the case of two couples who – for completely different reasons – were late arriving at the dock and therefore missed their reserved places on the *Herald of Free Enterprise* when she set sail. Some people actually swapped positions just before the disaster at the Hillsborough football stadium – the ones who would have been in the centre of the disaster area survived while those who would have been in a place of safety sadly died.

There was even the case of the elderly lady who miraculously survived a train crash in England a few years ago but became so depressed that her two sons decided to give her a special Christmas present and send her to visit her family in the United States. Her ticket was for the plane that crashed at Lockerbie.

If it is the case – and I truly believe there is sufficient evidence to show that it is – that our time to die has been prearranged, then how can you be in any way to blame for an accident to your child which was beyond your control? This does not mean, of course, that we should not all take as much care and attention as possible throughout our lives. It's no good thinking 'Oh well, I will only die when the time is right' and then taking foolish risks. If it isn't your time to die, you could be left horribly injured. So belief in predetermination of the moment of death does not absolve you of responsibility while alive.

If you were not present when your child died as the result of an accident, there is often an element of disbelief. 'They must have got it wrong', 'He'll be back soon', 'It must have been someone else'. Going to the scene of the accident – or as near as it is possible to go – is not being ghoulish for those who have been bereaved. For many people it helps to turn the situation from nightmare into reality – and, painful as it may be, reality must be faced if you are to begin your healing process.

Many parents who have lost children through accidents find comfort in trying to do something positive to ensure that their loss is not suffered by other mothers and fathers. Campaigning for a new zebra crossing or for increased safety regulations at a youth camp may not bring your child back but it does help you to believe that they did not die in vain and that their life, however brief, had great meaning and purpose and benefited others.

CRIME

Thankfully, whatever we read in the newspapers, the number of children who die as the result of criminal action is comparatively small – although even one would be one too many. The number however, is growing, which means that an increasing number of parents must live with the knowledge that their child's death was caused by the deliberate action of someone else. Sometimes this action is aimed at the individual child; at others it is the result of offences such as the tragically misnamed 'joyriding', where the unfortunate victim just happened to be the one in the way.

Parents of such children do not only have all the usual aspects of grief to cope with; they must also deal with their feelings towards the perpetrators of such crimes. It must be very easy for them to allow their minds and hearts to become filled with hatred and thoughts of vengeance, but in doing so they allow the criminal to steal the future not only from their child but from themselves as well.

There are innumerable instances of the lives of parents being torn apart after the death of a child as the result of crime – leading to divorce, violence or mental illness. There are also instances of those who have turned their personal tragedy to public good. Think of Diana Lamplugh whose daughter Suzy disappeared and is presumed dead after an encounter with a 'Mr Kipper'. Since that time her mother has shown remarkable strength of spirit and has thrown her considerable energies into teaching other young women how best to protect themselves. And what of Gordon Wilson whose beloved daughter died as the result of a bomb blast at Enniskillen? He could so easily have spent the rest of his life wallowing in a morass of hatred and vengeance. Instead he turned his attention to working in any way he could to help the peace process so that other fathers might be spared his anguish. Similarly, Colin Parry, the father of Tim, one of the two young boys killed by an IRA bomb in Warrington, has been campaigning for peace, seeing this as a more fitting tribute to his son's memory than constantly contemplating the devastating results of war.

These are just three of the many, many examples of brave parents who have determined to turn their personal tragedy into positive good for other children or for the world in general. How proud those children must be of them now.

Suppose those parents had not managed to turn their personal tragedy into good, what would have happened? It would have made no difference to their children who had so sadly died – but it would have made a great deal of difference both to them and to the world in general.

The world has benefited and will continue to benefit from the unselfishness and the dedication those bereaved parents are exhibiting. On an earthly level the parents themselves are working through their pain and grief and turning it to the advantage of other people's children – which is a form of therapy in itself. And spiritually they must have taken a giant step in their personal evolvement. Had they not done so – had they determined to concentrate on their anger, their hatred and their bitterness, what would have happened to them? They would certainly have suffered psychologically as well as physically as any negative emotion which is retained and brooded upon over a long period of time can only increase, and a body which is full of such negativity has to break down in some way. This in turn only increases the reasons for their anger and the whole vicious cycle starts all over again.

And that is without taking into account their spiritual health. If, as I suggested earlier, we are faced with potential 'lessons' in life but must choose for ourselves whether to learn them or not, surely someone who allows such bitterness to dominate their life – even with such good reason – is also setting themselves back spiritually.

Organ donation

One of the ways in which many parents who have tragically lost a child try to bring forth some good out of the bad is to permit the transplant of organs from their child's body. These organs can often be used to save the life of not just one but many other people.

One young mother whose nine-year-old daughter had

died as the result of a car accident told me that it helped her enormously to come to terms with her grief when she realized that her little girl had given sight to two people, had saved another child from the sentence of a lifetime on a kidney machine and had prevented the death of yet another whose heart and liver were defective. She said that she was so proud of her daughter for saving the health and lives of those people and – although her death was naturally a source of personal grief – in some ways it seemed that she had not died at all but still lived on in all those other people.

Many people are still hesitant about permitting the donation of organs from those who have died – especially their children – and yet, having spoken to many parents who have permitted this to be done, not one of them has ever regretted it and every one has felt that it gave special meaning to the life of their own child.

If your life is shattered by the loss of a beloved child – in whatever circumstances – here are a few pointers which may help you come to terms with what has happened.

- Try to think in terms of more than just what happens during this lifetime. Even if you do not understand *why* your child has been taken from you, it can help if you can accept that it is all part of some great spiritual plan which is beyond our comprehension.
- If you can accept that way of thinking, then your child must have been a highly evolved spirit if it had no need to remain on this earth for more than a short time.
- Put aside all feelings of self-blame. It is not your fault – whether this was a miscarriage, a cot death, an accident or any other tragedy. To fill yourself with guilt cannot bring your child back and can only do harm to you and those you love.
- It is important to talk. You may be tempted to shut yourself away from life – and particularly from contact with other people's children – but this can only do you harm. The longer you keep yourself in isolation, the

harder it will be to get back to living again. It doesn't matter whether you prefer to talk to family, friends or a trained counsellor, so long as you *do* talk.

- Try to understand your friends if they do not know what to say to you. Just by being there, they are showing you that their hearts and thoughts are with you. Don't shut them out.

- If you suffer a miscarriage, be sure to do something to commemorate your unborn child's life. If you are religious, then you will have various rituals which you may find helpful. But, even if you are not, something as simple as planting a tree or buying a teddy bear can provide physical evidence of your baby's existence.

- Remember that when you cry you are crying for yourself – and there is nothing wrong with that. But, whatever your beliefs, you child cannot now be suffering in any way.

- Take care of your health. You have been through the most stressful experience that can happen to anyone and such extremes of stress can cause a breakdown of physical and mental health. So be sure to get sufficient rest – even if sleep is difficult at first. See to it that you take care of your nutritional needs – using vitamin and mineral supplements if you feel you do not want to eat.

- If your child was not at home when she or he died, you may find it helps to come to terms with the reality of what has happened if you pay a deliberate visit to the place where it happened.

- If the death was caused by someone else – whether accidentally or deliberately – try not to allow yourself to become filled with hatred or thoughts of vengeance. Of course such feelings are quite understandable but they can do no good to the child you have lost and may well cripple you emotionally for the rest of your life.

- See what you can do to bring some good out of your own personal tragedy. Whether you start a fundraising organization, allow the donation of organs, or campaign for changes which will prevent other parents suffering as you have, keep the memory of your child alive in a way which brings maximum benefit to others.

- Realize that you have to go through all the stages of grief and that you must do so at your own pace. There is no 'correct' amount of time for grieving. But realize too that the greatest tribute you can pay to the memory of your child is, when you are ready, to go on with your life in as positive a way as possible – knowing that one day you will be together again.

CHAPTER 6

Special Cases

There is no form of bereavement which is easy to deal with and every death is a personal source of grief to someone. However, there are certain cases where that grief is magnified and intensified almost beyond tolerance.

SUICIDE

To know that someone you loved and cared about reached such a low point and became so desperate that the only recourse which appeared to them was to end their own life is almost beyond bearing. Although, as we have seen, a sense of guilt (justified or not) is involved in most cases of bereavement, nowhere is this stronger than in the case of bereavement by suicide. Those who grieve are left to ask themselves why they had not recognized the desperation in the person concerned or whether there was something they could have done to prevent it.

The very act of ending their own life deliberately means that the balance of that person's mind was upset, albeit possibly temporarily. Human instinct is for survival. You have only to think of the numbers of people who survived the horrors of concentration camps or who have managed to pull themselves back from the brink of death after some terrible illness or accident to realize that all human beings when acting and thinking normally will go to any lengths to survive.

If you can accept that premise and realize that the person who has committed suicide was not thinking normally at the time, then you must realize that there was nothing you could do to prevent it happening. You might possibly have succeeded in postponing it but if they remained determined they would have found a time and a place to try again.

I have only known one person, a very dear friend, who took his own life and I well remember my own feelings of guilt at the time. It was just a few years ago and he must have reached such a low pitch in his life that he decided not to continue. And this was no cry for help – he really meant to do it. He went to a place which he knew was deserted so that there was no possibility of him being found before the deed was done.

I had spoken to this friend on the telephone two days earlier. We had a long, pleasant conversation during which he sounded just as he always did. After hearing of the method of his death, I went over and over that conversation in my mind wondering whether I had missed signs of distress that I should have picked up, or whether there were words I could have used which would have caused him to change his mind. It took me quite some time to accept the fact that there was nothing I could have done. The person who spoke to me on the telephone that day was not the same person who chose to end his life just two days later.

There were others who had spent time with this man the day before the tragedy – and they too had noticed nothing untoward about his manner or words. What happened between the Saturday afternoon when all appeared normal and the early hours of Sunday morning when he drove to that isolated spot and fed a tube through the window from the exhaust of his car none of us will ever know. He left hastily scribbled notes, written on the Sunday morning, but they told us nothing except that – at that time – he was convinced that this was the right thing to do.

However much we love them and want the best for them, we cannot take responsibility for the actions of other adults – and you cannot be responsible for the action of someone terminating their life, even though you wish you could.

The only instance when such behaviour is understandable to many people is when a terminal illness has been diagnosed. I am not saying for a moment that this is the right thing to do – merely that it is something most of us can understand. No one wants to think that all they have to look forward to is a life of increasing debility accompanied perhaps by pain and total dependence on others. But there are so many people who have fought battles against such illnesses and won – often giving themselves months or even years of life which may be different to the life they led before but which still has great quality to it.

Think of Roy Castle, the British entertainer. He knew he was dying of lung cancer but he went on smiling and performing to the end. The 'extra time' he was allotted may not have been very long – but think what he did with it. Not only did he prove to the world that it was still possible to smile at times of such great adversity but he wrote personal letters of hope and inspiration to many other sufferers – some of whom had been ready to give up but who with Roy's help regained the will to live and (at the time of writing this) are still alive and experiencing a positive quality of life.

So accept that you are bound to experience some feelings of guilt if someone you love has taken their own life. But then, as we have seen, most people who have been bereaved feel guilty about something – this is a normal part of the grieving process. Eventually you have to let that guilt go and accept that it was up to the individual to decide at that unbalanced moment what to do.

The other emotion which accompanies the suicide of someone close is anger. I can well remember feeling this about my friend. How dare he cause such grief to his family and his friends! What a cruel and selfish act it seemed to be to think only of his own feelings and not of those whose lives he was destroying in the process.

But I soon realized that this emotion too was pointless. The kind and compassionate man I had known for years would never have hurt anyone deliberately, particularly the members of his immediate family to whom he was very close. But the person who took his life on that chilly Sunday morning was not the man I had known for years. He was different because of the effects of the mental disturbance he was experiencing at the time. So who was it that I was angry with? Not my friend, but a total stranger.

At least you can realize that whatever the mental torment that person was experiencing she or he is now at peace. Whether you believe that nothing exists after this life or that there is another place for us to go to, there will be an end to all suffering – physical or mental.

And, if you accept the theory that your spirit chooses the moment of death from the very beginning of your life (even if not the method of that death), then there was nothing you could have done to prevent that life ending on that day.

If the person who committed suicide made a choice on the day of their death, you have a choice to make afterwards. You can choose to spend the rest of your life brooding about what they did and tormenting yourself with thoughts of 'if only'. Or you can accept that at the moment they ended their life, they were not really the person you knew, and make every effort to remember them in the happier times – as I am sure they would prefer to be remembered. Whatever you decide, you can neither help nor hurt the one who has died – but you can certainly affect the whole of your life (and therefore the lives of all those around you) for years to come.

So send out thoughts or prayers for the healing of their spirit and for them to be able to find peace wherever they are now, and concentrate on all the good times when they were their real selves.

LOSING YOUR PARTNER

Finding yourself left alone without a beloved partner – whether you were together for four months or 40 years – can be devastating. In addition to the grief, there are so many practical things to attend to and sometimes the responsibility of coping with it all can seem too great.

The problems which arise may vary – often according to the age group of the widowed partner – but each brings difficulty in its wake.

For those of the older generation, there are the practicalities of dealing with everyday life. Things have changed considerably over the years but there are still many older people who were brought up at a time when the man took care of the finances and the bills while the woman was responsible for running the home and preparing the meals.

I have known several cases of women in their 70s who suddenly found themselves for the first time having to cope with cheque books, insurance policies and financial decisions – and to whom this was terrifying and extremely stressful.

Many men of that age have no idea how to work the washing machine or prepare nutritious meals for themselves and often because they do not want to appear foolish they hesitate to ask anyone for assistance.

If either of the above situations applies to you, please do not delay asking for help – whether from a friend, a member of the family or (particularly in the case of finances) from a professional. Coping with the death of a partner is difficult enough without all these extra problems. And they can be overcome so quickly and easily. You will only need to be shown once how to write a cheque or work the washing machine and you will be able to do it ever afterwards. So why go on suffering and adding to the problems you already have?

Those who have a large house or one which requires both salaries to keep up may wonder whether they will be able to go on living in their own home or whether they are to lose that too. Even if you have no mortgage on your home or have the type of policy which ensures that a mortgage is paid in full on the death of one partner, there is still the maintenance and upkeep to be considered. And only one salary to do it on.

If this applies to you, then do seek proper advice as soon as possible. Things are often not as bad as they might at first seem and you could save yourself many a sleepless night by finding out just where you stand.

Lizzie was naturally devastated when Malcolm died suddenly after a comparatively short illness. They had always enjoyed a good lifestyle, living in a large house in the suburbs and sending their two teenage sons to private school. An insurance policy ensured that the mortgage on the house was immediately paid up on Malcolm's death and another gave Lizzie what appeared at first to be a generous amount of money.

When she started to do her calculations however Lizzie became increasingly worried. She had not been working outside the home for some years and although she might be fortunate enough to get some sort of job it would certainly not be something which provided a large salary. There might be no mortgage but there was still the upkeep of the house to consider – including decorating, heating, tending the extensive gardens. The boys' school fees seemed to increase with each year and on top of that she had to find money for all the 'extras' – uniform, school outings and so on. While this would be difficult, Lizzie did not want her sons to feel that lack of funds was preventing them from doing all the things their friends were doing.

So, on top of her grief at Malcolm's death and having to cope with her sons' emotions at this difficult time, Lizzie became increasingly worried about money. Not wanting to traumatize the boys still further by uprooting them from the only home they had ever known, she decided to say nothing but to do her best to manage her finances in such a way that she would be able to keep going as before.

As month followed expensive month, the stress of coping on her own with her financial problems caused Lizzie great distress. This was not made easier by the fact that, with the boys away and not really being in the mood for socializing, she now spent much of the time on her own. This gave her time to think and once that thinking became negative there was no one there to talk her out of it. Eventually she became quite ill, unable to eat or sleep – and this caused her to worry even more: who would look after the boys if anything happened to her?

Finally Lizzie did what she should have done right at the start. She went to see Malcolm's accountant and the family solicitor. She explained the whole situation to them and asked for their advice. The outcome was that she decided to sell the big house and move to something smaller which she could buy outright. She was therefore able to invest the difference in the house values in something which gave her a reasonable amount of interest – and a great deal of peace of mind.

The boys were not nearly as upset at the move as Lizzie had feared they would be. For one thing, teenage boys are not usually terribly concerned about the differences between one house and another and, for another, they were away at school for the greater part of the time.

If your grief at the loss of your partner is made even worse by worries concerning your home, your general finances or your children, it is important to seek outside professional help from someone you feel you can trust. The last thing you need is extra pressures at a time when your own emotions may be making it more difficult than usual for you to think clearly and logically.

Another person often greatly affected by financial worries is the woman who is widowed while still quite young. Because of the vagaries of the current British pension system, a woman under the age of 45 does not qualify for a widow's pension (although with dependent children she can apply for the widowed mother's allowance).

When I was widowed in 1982 the qualifying age was 40. Although, naturally, I was pleased to receive the widow's pension (such as it is), my sons were by then in their late teens which meant that I was able to work full time without worrying about child minders, nurseries, playgroups and so on.

In that same year a friend of mind was also widowed. She was 28 years old, had a two-year-old son and was six months pregnant when her husband suddenly collapsed and died at work. She was not entitled to the widow's pension but was in no position to get a job. The widowed mother's allowance she received was not generous and she had to apply for and claim supplementary benefits from the appropriate departments.

The additional benefits she received made life somewhat easier – although they certainly did not make her rich! But remember she had to make all these claims and worry about her finances at a time when she had just lost her husband and was about to have a baby. When I spoke to her she was extremely upset saying that she felt she was going to have to spend the next few years living 'on charity handouts'.

If you find, whatever your age and situation, that you are unable to manage financially without state assistance, please don't hesitate to apply for it. It is *not* charity. It is something we all contribute to all our working lives in order that those in need will not suffer. It is not – and probably never will be – generous but it is your entitlement and receiving it can help to alleviate at least some of the anxieties you are experiencing at your time of grief.

(By the way, my friend's story had a happy ending. Four years later she married a delightful man who adores her, her two children and the two who were born as a result of their marriage.)

Of course the worries widows and widowers experience are not all concerned with finance. Whatever their age and circumstances, they have to wonder whether they are going to spend the rest of their life alone and without a partner.

At the time of their bereavement most people insist that they will never marry or live with anyone again. For one thing it seems disloyal to the person they have just lost, and for another the fear of experiencing the same sort of hurt again in the future is intolerable. But as time passes and life begins to return to normal, it is quite natural for their thoughts to turn to the future and the possibility of another partner.

Some people, of course, will come to the conclusion that they do not wish to share their life with anyone in the future but prefer to live alone. This is fine provided it is by choice and they are happy to do so. Others, however, will feel that their life is not complete with a spouse or partner. This is fine too – and in many cases a tribute to the person they have lost. They are not trying to 'replace' this person but, having experienced one good relationship, would like the opportunity of doing so again.

The trouble is that it is not that easy to meet potential partners once you are past the disco and nightclub phase of your life. Where do you go? The best thing is to go somewhere where you will meet new people of both sexes rather than to appear to be 'partner hunting'. I am sure that some men and women meet the partner of their dreams through a dating agency or singles club – but it is the most unnatural way of going about it.

Think about what normally happens when a man and woman meet in less contrived circumstances. The conversation is general, they have time to get to know one another slowly and to find out what they have in common and what they do not. If you have just paid a handsome sum of money to an agency in order to be introduced to a certain number of potential partners, then, from the very first meeting, that is how you are going to be considering each other. It won't be a case of 'this is a person I would like to get to know' but 'would she/he make a suitable life partner for me?' So the vital stage of acquaintanceship is missed out altogether.

I am not criticizing such agencies. The numbers of people they have on their books (although obviously not all widows and widowers) indicate that there are people who feel that this is the way for them. But the numbers of people who either leave the agency dissatisfied or remain on their books for a considerable time show that it is certainly not the answer in every case.

So where does the widowed man or woman go to meet new people? The best answer is probably to find some place where you can meet others with whom you already share an interest. If you are interested in a particular hobby – from cactus plants to photography, from ice skating to dog breeding – there are clubs, societies and organizations to cater for your interests. If you do not have a specific hobby as yet, you might like to join an evening class and study any topic which appeals to you. If you do this for your own interest and to meet new people in general, you will certainly enhance your own life and make a new circle of acquaintances and perhaps friends. If you do meet someone there with whom you eventually become emotionally involved, that is a bonus.

Perhaps more than any other group of bereaved people, those who have been widowed tend to suffer pangs of guilt the first time they find themselves laughing again, kissing again or having sex again. And the longer they have been together with their partner, the more intensely this guilt seems to be felt. But imagine things had been the other way around. Suppose you had been the one to die, leaving behind you the partner you truly loved. Would you really want to think of that person living a permanently solitary life, avoiding the possibility of any deep and meaningful relationship in the future? I think not. You would want them to be happy and to live a full and fruitful life again.

If this is what you would want for your partner if you were the one to die, isn't it something of an insult to their memory to assume that she or he would want any less for you? Of course you may choose, for your own reasons, not to become emotionally involved again – and that is your right. The tragedy would be if you really wanted another relationship but allowed guilt or misguided loyalty to hold you back.

Widowed people often find it quite difficult to join in life again once their immediate grief has subsided. They often feel uncomfortable going on holiday alone or feeling that they are the 'odd one out' at some social occasion. But this need not be the case as things are not the same as they used to be many years ago: there are many people on their own. Sometimes this is through personal choice, sometimes as the result of a divorce or separation. Indeed, there are now more people living, socializing and travelling on their own than there have ever been.

So far as holidays are concerned, there are organizations which specialize in vacations for single people from the 18 to 30 clubs for younger people to SAGA for those who are older. So, whether you prefer to travel alone, with a friend or with a large and organized group, your needs are provided for.

VICTIMS OF CRIME

As touched on in Chapter 5, those who have lost someone as a result of criminal action on the part of a third party have to contend with an enormous amount of anger in addition to all the other emotions they are experiencing. The anger may be directed at the individual or people concerned or be because of the senseless waste of a precious life.

Some crimes of violence which end in the loss of life are deliberately aimed at those who become the victims but many appear to be the result of someone being in the wrong place at the wrong time and this is where recriminations (against yourself or others) come to the fore. 'If only I had told him to be home earlier...' 'She wouldn't have gone out at all if you hadn't had that row with her...' 'I shouldn't have let her go on her own.'

Such recriminations only serve to fuel the burning anger. And they achieve nothing. What has happened, has happened. All the 'if onlys' in the world cannot change it. If you believe that the moment of death is selected by our spirits, then *something* was bound to happen on that day to the person concerned. Even if you cannot accept this, you do nothing to bring back the person you mourn nor do you allow yourself to mourn them properly by filling your heart and mind with rage.

Because I have the good fortune not to have been in the position of losing someone in that way I can of course only speak as an onlooker. But I have counselled many people over the years who *have* experienced this type of loss and I can assure you from my work with such people that it is only those who are able at some point to let their anger go who are able to go on and lead their lives in a normal and positive way.

You may have read in the papers of people who have reacted in extreme ways after losing someone as a result of violent crime. There are those who are still consumed with hatred and vowing revenge upon the perpetrator of the crime should they ever manage to take it even 20 years afterwards. I fully understand and sympathize with someone who feels like this but if you look at their lives over those past years you will find a history of bitterness, marriage breakdown and ill-health. This has done nothing to harm the criminal (whether in custody or not) – and certainly nothing to help the grieving sufferer who has been living a life of torment. In addition, instead of being able to remember the good things about the one they loved and so tragically lost, that memory now is marred and tainted by years of bitterness and hate.

At the other end of the scale, I remember reading some time ago about a grieving mother whose child had been killed in a 'joyriding' incident. This woman actually found the strength to go to the prison where the perpetrator was being held, to visit him and to tell him that she forgave him.

I have to be honest here and say that I do not know if I would have been able to do as that mother did. It must have taken an enormous amount of courage and strength of will to confront her daughter's killer in that way and to offer him forgiveness. But not only did she cleanse herself of the harmful effects of long-held hate, she enabled her daughter's memory to remain untainted by bitterness and thoughts of vengeance.

For most people the answer would lie somewhere between those two extremes. If you allow hate for the perpetrator of the crime to build up within you to such an extent that it colours the whole of your life, surely you are in danger of bringing yourself down to their level. I am not saying that you should not want them imprisoned – possibly for a very long time – but that is society's vengeance, not yours.

In some cases, of course, there is not even the satisfaction of a suitable prison sentence. Sometimes the perpetrator is not caught at all, sometimes she or he is given a ridiculously short sentence – or even acquitted altogether because of lack of evidence. Even if this happens, don't allow your anger to damage the remainder of your life and destroy what should be the good memories of the times you shared with the person you have lost.

Anger and hatred are forms of negative energy and as such can be totally destructive to the sufferer while achieving nothing beneficial. Your anger will not make a prison sentence one day longer. The criminal will either be remorseful or will not – your anger is not going to change that. Your anger will not bring back the person for whom you grieve. All it will do is fill your being with negative energy, leaving little or no room for anything that is positive or good, and your life will become meaningless.

Why not turn that energy into something positive? Depending upon the circumstances of your own particular tragedy, you might campaign for better street lighting, stricter firearm laws or tougher prison sentences. At least you will be using your accumulated energy for a good purpose. It may be too late to help your own particular victim but you may help to prevent other people becoming victims or to make the lives of those who lose loved ones more bearable. And in this way the death of the one you loved will have been for a purpose rather than a complete waste.

After a death caused by crime you will probably be contacted by someone from a victim support agency. Even if you feel that you want to be left alone in your grief, I would urge you to allow them to help you. Not only are they well trained in the special counselling needed at such times, but they will deal with many of the practicalities with which you may not be able to cope. They will attend court either with you or in your place and will often liaise between you and the police. They will also remain in contact with you for as long as you need it – even if this is some time after matters appear to have been brought to a close.

I have called this chapter 'Special Cases' – but of course every bereavement is special to the person who suffers it. If your loss falls into one of the categories described in this chapter, you will experience all the emotions which always accompany bereavement but often to a heightened degree.

CHAPTER 7

When You Have Time

It can be devastating to be told that someone for whom you care deeply has been given only a limited time to live. No one wants to hear this and the news is bound to be followed by a period of mixed emotions – including grief, disbelief, anger, fear and anxiety. Once this stage has passed, however, you might be able to realize that there are some positive aspects to this advance knowledge.

When someone who is seemingly healthy suddenly dies with no warning signs, those who grieve for them are faced not only with many practical difficulties but also with many emotional ones. The guilt which we now know accompanies almost every bereavement is often increased because suddenly there is no time to put right any differences or clear up any misunderstandings. Life becomes a series of 'if onlys': 'If only I had telephoned when I meant to.' 'If only I had come to see him.' 'If only I had apologized for that silly argument'.

When you are given time to put right all the wrongs and to say all those things you really want to say, you can minimize the amount of guilt you experience and can help yourself to deal with the death when it comes by remembering that you had the opportunity to clear the air of any misunderstandings which might previously have existed.

Sometimes, of course, the person themselves might not have been told of the seriousness of their condition. Although it is widely believed today that it is best to be completely honest with every patient, there are still some doctors – and I have to say that I agree with them – who pause to take into account the ability of the individual to cope with that knowledge. While one person will want to know the truth of the situation so that they can put up a fight – even winning it as has happened in many reported cases – there are others who would be so aghast at the news and so ready to accept the inevitability of the diagnosis that they would almost be inclined to sit back and wait for the moment of death.

I know of one case where an elderly lady – who had always been a nervous type and had suffered from panic attacks throughout her life – developed a cancerous tumour. Her son, with whom she lived, knew perfectly well that if his mother were to be told the truth she would become so distressed that she could immediately weaken her physical condition. Not only that but his mother was of a generation where doctors were looked on as all-powerful beings who could never be wrong so it would not occur to her to question his words or the accuracy of any stated prognosis. He therefore begged the doctor not to let his mother know the precise truth of her situation – and the doctor agreed. Naturally the woman knew that she was ill and that she had to have an operation but when surgery was over she was told that the reason for her illness had now been completely removed and that she had merely to regain her strength. This she did and, although she only lived for a further two years, they were two good years which she was able to enjoy with her children and grandchildren.

Let's suppose, however, that both you and the patient know perfectly well that the condition from which she or he is suffering is terminal. Having been given that knowledge, you have also been granted a period of time to talk together, to discuss your mutual hopes and fears, to express your love and to put right any wrongs which may have occurred between you.

Be sure you make the most of that time. Too many people skirt around the subject of the illness or don't mention it at all – and this can be highly distressing to the person who is ill. It is not that she or he wants to talk about it all the time but neither do they want it ignored completely.

Roger was in his early 30s when he came to see me. He had cancer which had spread to several organs and had been told that he had about a year to live. The reason he came to see me was to help with the control of the pain which (fortunately) he only experienced intermittently. After the initial emotional period, he had accepted the reality of his condition and its outcome – although he hoped that the doctors were being pessimistic in their prognosis of the time he had left.

We talked a great deal as we worked together and there were two things uppermost in Roger's mind. The first was – in his words – that he wanted to 'really live until I die'. In other words, he wanted to make the most of every moment he had left and to do as many as possible of the things he had always wanted to do. These varied from riding a horse to going in a hot air balloon and being at Wembley for the cup final.

The other thing Roger desperately wanted was to be able to talk to his parents and sister about what was happening to him. But they were still in a state of complete denial and refused to accept what the doctors had said or that the son and brother they loved only had a limited life span left. This made Roger feel that he was fighting his battles all on his own instead of having the support and backing of his family.

With his permission, I arranged to meet Roger's parents and sister and explained to them how he was feeling. They had not realized they were causing him distress but had thought that by pretending that nothing was wrong they were enabling him to live a more 'normal' life. It was a highly emotional occasion but it was effective. The next time I saw Roger he told me that he and his family had sat up late into one night discussing the future and what they were going to do in order to make best use of the time he had left.

If someone you love has been given a limited future, it

is also important to talk together about the moment of death itself and what they and you think happens afterwards. This is not being morbid or miserable – they are thoughts that will be going round in everyone's head anyway. Try and find out what is the greatest fear in the mind of the patient. Some are afraid of the 'nothing' which they think comes after death while others, like a colleague of mine who died about six years ago, worry about the last days. As this colleague said to me: 'I'm not scared of being dead – just of how I get there.'

Once you know what the greatest fear is, it might be possible to alleviate it. If the fear is of pain, ask a professional to explain what will be done to minimize this. If it is of what comes after death, spend some time talking about what each of you believe. There are many examples and books detailing near-death experiences which can be read and not one of these describes it in horrific terms. On the contrary, the pain and discomfort only seem to arise when the person who has almost died is revived.

If the person who is ill already has a religious belief or is searching for one, make time for discussion and exploration of various ideas and philosophies. If they have no belief at all, this too can be discussed.

I have worked with many people who knew perfectly well that they had only a limited time left in which to live. To almost every one it was important to have a chance to express their wishes about what was to happen after their death – whether the type of funeral they wished to have or who was to have some precious possession. All too often, loving and distressed families try to dissuade them from talking about such things by telling them that 'there's plenty of time to think about that'. But the patient knows that this is just not true and really feels the need to sort out as many matters as possible before it is too late.

If you are in such a situation with someone you love, remember that discussing what they want to happen after their death will not hasten that event any more than the making of a will causes an otherwise healthy person to fall

ill and die. At all times, however, try and follow the lead
of the person themselves and talk about those things *they*
want to talk about.

Another thing they might well want to discuss is *your*
general plans for the future. It would be easy to think
that they would not want to consider what is going to
happen in the world after they have left it – but this is very
rarely the case. It often helps to give a sense of purpose
and continuity to life in general to know that those
they leave behind have hopes, plans and dreams for the
future.

There are disagreements and rifts at some point in most
close relationships and perhaps the greatest gift given by
the awareness of a finite amount of time left is the opportunity to put these right.

When Alison was very small, she and her father were
very close. Having three older brothers she was always
'daddy's girl'. As she grew up, however, they experienced
many difficulties. George came from a very poor background but was determined that all his children would
have the best possible education which could be provided
so that they would all have the opportunity to make the
most of themselves.

All four went to university. Alison had only been there
18 months when she informed her father that she intended
to drop out and marry the young man she had been seeing. The young man in question was a singer in a pop
group and Alison intended to travel the country with him.
George was horrified that his daughter was – as he saw it
– throwing away all her opportunities to follow some
worthless fellow from place to place when he would probably discard her when he grew tired of her. Unfortunately
he did not merely voice his views to his daughter, he actually forbade her to do as she intended and told her that the
young man would never be welcome in his home.

Alison's reponse was – unsurprisingly – that if her
future husband was not welcome then she obviously was
not welcome either. Father and daughter parted on

extremely bad terms and George and his wife were not present at the wedding ceremony which followed shortly afterwards.

The marriage lasted about seven years during which time there was absolutely no contact between George and Alison, even though she gave birth to two daughters. When her husband finally left her for another woman, Alison felt that could not possibly get in touch with her father because all he would say was that he had 'told her so'. In addition, she had been left in difficult financial circumstances and did not want to give George the opportunity to say that she only came back to him when she needed help.

Year followed year and, as each of them had the opportunity to think about the past and what they perceived as the negative behaviour of the other, the rift between them grew ever wider. Eventually, when Alison's daughters were in their teens and she had got herself a good job where she had worked hard to make progress, George became terminally ill. His family spent a great deal of time with him and, although they may have guessed that he was longing to see his daughter again, something – whether pride, stubbornness or fear of rejection – prevented him from asking for her.

Finally his wife and sons decided to try and trace Alison, which they did without too much difficulty. Her immediate reaction was to want to be with her father – even though she was frightened that he might not want to see her. She made her way to the hospital and, to everyone's joy, there was a happy and emotional reunion.

They did not waste time on recriminations about the past or talking about who was wrong and who was right. In the time he had left, George and Alison were able to rekindle the love they had always had for each other and he also had the chance to get to know the two granddaughters he had never seen.

After George's death Alison naturally experienced a measure of guilt about the fact that she and her father had been apart for so long. But think how much greater that guilt would have been if she had never been reunited with him. She was also able to remember the very genuine joy of her father when he met his granddaughters for the first time.

There was no proof that George's health was in any way improved by the reunion with his daughter and meeting with her children – but it certainly would not have been made worse. There is much documented evidence to show how greatly the body is affected by the mind and the anger, sorrow and bitterness George must have been experiencing cannot have helped but contribute to the deterioration of his health. Equally, the joy he felt when the reunion took place may well have extended his life – or at any rate the quality of that life. What greater gift could a daughter give the father who, although he may have gone about things in the wrong way, was probably doing what he considered to be in her best interests at the time?

The rift between two people is not always as total and dramatic as that between George and Alison. Sometimes there is a relatively minor bone of contention which nonetheless has damaged what would otherwise be strong and good. Even if it is a matter no one talks about, it remains there as a dangerous undercurrent lurking in the depths of their relationship.

Whatever differences of opinion you may have had in the past – great or small – make best use of the time you have been given to make up for them. Don't worry at this point about who was right – it changes nothing and serves no purpose.

There are many friends and family members where the relationship has always been fine but no one has ever actually said what they feel. This could be because something in their early background made them grow into people who do not easily express their feelings. Or it could be that because the other person is undemonstrative, you in turn find it difficult or embarrassing to show your feelings to them.

Think back to when you were a small child. When you were unhappy, hurt or frightened, what was it that made you feel better? A hug, a kiss, tender words – these could do so much, even when the situation was irreparable and a favourite toy was broken or a treasured childhood possession lost. We don't grow out of needing hugs, kisses and tender words – although most of us are afraid of asking for them. If the person you love is hurting, whether physically or emotionally, or if they are scared, you may not actually be able to cure their illness by putting your arms around them and reassuring them of your love but you will help them to feel secure and protected and will give them the strength to go on and face whatever the future holds for them.

If you are someone who has always found spontaneous expression of your feelings difficult, try not to let this prevent you speaking from your heart now. I promise you that to the person who most needs to hear the words it will not sound trite or foolish. Don't plan or rehearse what you want to say; let it be as spontaneous as possible. In that way you will instinctively select the right words and the right accompanying actions.

Some people are confined to bed as their condition deteriorates but there are many others who have not yet reached that stage but who still know what the prognosis is. These people will vary enormously as to what they want and how they wish to spend their remaining time. While one will want to be in their own home for as long as possible, surrounded by familiar things and people, others will determine to cram into their remaining time as many unfulfilled ambitions as possible.

Roger was one of these. You may recall that among his ambitions were the desires to fly in a hot air balloon, ride a horse and go to Wembley for the cup final. He also wanted to see the Lake District at daffodil time and learn to play the guitar. At first his parents did all they could to persuade him to set these ambitions aside in the hope that by doing so he would lengthen his life by a few weeks.

Eventually, however, Roger was able to persuade them that simply existing for a longer period of time was not enough if that time was to stand empty and barren. He knew that his physical condition would make many of the things he wanted to do tiring but he was prepared to rest before and afterwards to make them possible. What he did not want was to end his life without having anything to look forward to.

Roger managed to fulfil all but one of his ambitions. Sadly his life ended before the date of the cup final so he never got to Wembley. But he already had his ticket and was looking forward to being there when the end came and so his last weeks and months were spent fulfilling ambitions and looking forwards. When I spoke to his parents some time after his death, they told me that they were truly happy that Roger had been able to do so many ot the things he had always wanted to.

People who know that they are terminally ill seem to develop an inner strength and serenity which is denied to the rest of us. Whatever their initial reaction to the news, once they have come to terms with the knowledge, they seem in many cases to become peaceful and accepting – not in a hopeless and fatalistic way but in a positive sense as though they know they are progressing towards a place where they will be free and whole again.

This can be greatly helped by those around them – whether they are professional carers or loving friends or relatives. I have to admit that the first time I visited a hospice I was terrified. The thought of going into a place where everyone was 'waiting to die' made me extremely anxious. What would I say? How would I react?

I need not have worried. I have seldom been to a place where the atmosphere was so peaceful, loving and positive. Even the children, many of whom were confined to bed, exuded a serenity beyond their years. Friends and family came and went, the wonderful carers went about their work and – surprisingly to me at the time – the place rang with the sound of laughter. This was not the sorrowing place I had expected to find – and I have never been afraid of entering a hospice since that time.

So if someone you know has been told that they are terminally ill and been given an estimated future, look on it as an opportunity not granted to many and take advantage of the situation. With that knowledge you can do what you can to make the remainder of their life as positive and happy as possible and, as a result, you will know that you have given them the most precious of gifts – positive evidence of your love for them.

CHAPTER 8

Celebrate Life

Immediately after the death of someone close to you, you are naturally going to feel sad and experience all those other emotions which form a natural part of the grieving process. Eventually, however, the extremes of pain and distress depart and you have to face getting on with the rest of your life without their physical presence.

You will find yourself having to choose between two roads forward. Either you can be like Queen Victoria after the death of Prince Albert and elect to spend the rest of your life in mourning. Or you can learn to put the self-centredness of your grief behind you and go forwards as best you can. This does not mean that you are trying to eradicate the memory of the person who has died. Far from it. What you will be doing is keeping alive their memory in such a way that they are remembered with pleasure for who and what they were.

Instead of spending your time thinking of what you have lost and regretting all those things you never had, why not pay the person who has died the great compliment of remembering with pleasure all the good things about them and the times you shared?

For how does anyone continue to live once they have been released from their physical body? They continue to live by being remembered by other people. If no one ever thinks of them, it is almost as though they never existed or that their life served no purpose. And if every time they are remembered the occasion is a solemn one, accompanied by tears and sombre thoughts, eventually it is going to appear as if they were sombre and austere people who did not know how to have a good time.

Think about yourself. If you were to die tomorrow, would you prefer your friends and loved ones to cry and look gloomy every time your name was mentioned or would it make you happier to know that they were talking about you with warmth and affection – even smiling at the thought of the good times you shared? I know which I would prefer. Surely we can do as much for those we love.

Derek and Elaine had only been married for five years when she was tragically killed in an accident. Naturally the young man was greatly distressed and went through all the normal stages of the grieving process. So too did Elaine's many friends and relatives. They were all quite surprised, therefore, on the occasion of what would have been Elaine's next birthday, to receive invitations from Derek to a party to celebrate her life.

The party was a happy and joyous occasion with good music, food and wine. Everyone there naturally spoke of Elaine but not in the hushed and reverent tones often applied to someone who had died just months before. There was laughter as they remembered her fun and her happy-go-lucky attitude to life. There were fond recollections of her kindness and the way she had been ready to help so many people in any way she could. Old photographs were produced and handed round – Elaine as a baby, Elaine at school, Elaine in her student days, Elaine the bride.

By the end of the evening there was a beautiful atmosphere in the house Derek and Elaine had shared during their short married life. And, as each person left the party, it was with a smile and happy thoughts of the lovely young woman they used to know.

When speaking later of his decision to hold the party, Derek said that he had not wished the occasion of Elaine's birthday to pass unmarked but, at the same time, he knew that she would not want people to be miserable when thinking about her. He had asked himself what Elaine

would have liked had she lived and had then carried out
what he knew would be her wishes. He was pleased that
he had made all the guests feel happy, that he had felt
happy himself and, most important of all, that he believed
he had made Elaine feel happy too. He did not know what
he believed about life after death but he knew that Elaine
was 'somewhere' and that, from that somewhere she had
been able to see all her friends and relatives remembering
her with love and joy.

Some people, of course, will prefer a far more private
form of remembrance – and this is fine too. But, before you
do anything at all, stop and ask yourself why you feel the
need to commemorate the life which has ended. There will
probably be two reasons; the first is to make the loss easier
for you to bear and the second is to do something for the
person who has died.

There is nothing wrong in what some may see as the
'selfish' aspect of this. The death has occurred, you have
suffered the loss of someone you love. Why then should
you not do what you can to make that loss easier to deal
with? But how much more fulfilling it will be – and what a
fitting tribute to the person who has died – if that com-
memoration of their life is something they would have
enjoyed or wanted for themselves.

Here are just a few suggestions of ways in which a life
can be celebrated and remembered – but I'm sure you can
think of others for yourself.

PLANTING A TREE OR A BUSH

There is something very satisfying about using plants to
commemorate a life. Perhaps it is the fact that plants themselves are living things and that they go on from year to
year, and this helps us to believe in the continuity of life.
A perennial plant, whether a tree, shrub or bulb, will have
a period of the year when it appears to be dead, only to

spring into life again when the appropriate conditions prevail. Whatever your beliefs about the life which follows this one, you cannot fail to be uplifted when that special plant begins to live again – even if you are only aware of it on a subconscious level.

One man whose wife died of cancer planted an entire rose garden in her memory. She had loved roses and they were fortunate enough to have a large garden so in a warm and sunny spot he planted a dozen scented roses among which he placed a wooden seat. Sometimes, feeling the need to be close to his beloved wife again, he would sit there and silently tell her about his day. At others he simply enjoyed the flowers blooming around him. Whenever he sat on that seat among the blossoming roses he felt at peace.

Even if you do not have a garden of your own, you can place a plant in an existing garden – perhaps that of a friend or within a churchyard. Or you could plant a tree or bush in a piece of open land as long as it is not in a situation where it would cause problems to anyone else.

LIGHTING CANDLES

For as long as they have been in existence, candles have had a special significance to those who followed a specific religion as well as to those who did not. Whether or not you follow an orthodox religion, you will still be able to gain personal benefit from the lighting of a candle and taking the time immediately afterwards to establish your own method of communication with the person who has died. You may choose to speak to them aloud, to relax and think your own thoughts or to remember good times you shared. And I truly believe that, whether you are always aware of it or not, if you establish this sort of routine, the spirit of the one you have lost will be aware of what you are doing and will come closer to you.

RELIGIOUS RITUAL

If you are a follower of a particular religion, you will probably be able to find comfort in the rituals of your faith. Just make sure that you do not carry them out mechanically or that you do not use them as a time for re-emphasizing your grief. Let all memories be of the good times shared with the one you have lost rather than the sadness of their passing.

PICTURES – REAL AND IMAGINED

Some people find it helpful to talk to a photograph as it keeps the mind focused on the physical appearance of the person who has died. And since photographs are usually taken at happy times this can also help to dispel the gloomy thoughts associated with death and replace them with more positive ones of shared memories.

Even if you do not have a photograph, you can conjure up a picture in your imagination. Don't worry if at first the only image which appears is of the person as they were as they approached the end of their life. This is quite natural and will pass spontaneously.

My husband was the first dead person I had ever seen. For some months afterwards, whatever aspect of our life together I was thinking about, I could only picture him as he was immediately after his fatal heart attack. But after a few months I found that the image of him which came to mind was of him when he was fit, well and happy. I did not actually do anything to change this image – in fact, I only noticed the change some time after it had happened – but, perhaps for that very reason, it brought me a good deal of comfort.

One of things many people find extremely difficult is carrying out the necessary task of sorting through the belongings of someone after they have died – and the closer you were to them, the harder this seems to be. To see someone's life reduced to a selection of possessions can be very distressing. And yet, even these possessions are in a way a celebration of the life of the person concerned.

The value of the possessions has nothing to do with this celebration. Someone who was very rich may have amassed a collected of priceless objects and paintings simply because of their value and without having any real love for them in themselves. Another – less well off – may have accumulated during their lifetime a hotch-potch of items, none of which may have great commercial value but each of which was a source of great joy to them. Whether we are talking about a humble collection of picture postcards or an assortment of china knick-knacks given with love by children and grandchildren, those items are in their own way a celebration of the life of the person who owned them.

Bereaved people often do not know what to do with all these possessions. It is impossible to keep everything and yet there is frequently a sense of guilt at getting rid of them. This should not be the case. You do not have to keep all those things in order to remember the person who has died. The greatest and most elaborate shrine will not make you think more often or more lovingly of the one you have lost. Perhaps the best thing is to select one or two items of sentimental value you wish to keep – allowing others who were equally close to do the same – and then do whatever seems most fitting with what is left. In my house now I have my grandmother's china jam pot and mixing bowl, my father's leather-bound book of Shakespeare and his paper knife, and a little yew table which was my husband's, as well as all the birthday and anniversary cards he sent me. I also have lots of photographs of them all, and a multitude of loving, happy memories which all the treasures in the world could not enhance.

If those things which are left can do some good to someone else – either by being donated to charity or being sold and the money being used as the person would have appreciated – then this too is a celebration of their life. It is a means of allowing their kindness to continue after their death.

Remember that when we weep, we weep for ourselves because we are the ones left behind and we have lost someone very special to us. But there comes a time when the weeping stops and we realize that we are doing far more to honour their memory if we can find ways of celebrating their life.

CONCLUSION

The following was sent to me by a friend after the death of my husband and I found it gave me great comfort. I have since sent it to others who have been bereaved and they have found the same. I offer it to you in the hope that it might help you too. It is taken from a sermon preached by Henry Scott Holland on Whit Sunday, 1910:

Death is nothing at all. I have only slipped away into the next room.

I am I, and you are you. Whatever we were to each other, that we are still.

Call me by my old familiar name. Speak to me in the easy way which you always used.

Put no difference into your tone. Wear no forced air of solemnity or sorrow.

Laugh as we always laughed at the little jokes we enjoyed together.

Play...smile...think of me...pray for me.

Let my name be ever the household word that it always was.

Let it be spoken without effect, without a ghost of a shadow on it.

Life means all that it ever meant. It is the same as it ever was.

There is absolutely unbroken continuity.

What is this death but a negligible accident?

Why should I be out of mind because I am out of sight?

I am but waiting for you – for an interval.

Somewhere very near – just around the corner.

All is well.

Further Reading

Elisabeth Kubler-Ross, *On Death and Dying*, Tavistock/Routledge, 1970
Elisabeth Kubler-Ross, *On Children and Death*, Macmillan, 1985
Ursula Markham, *Women and Guilt*, Piatkus, 1995
Dr Donald Scott, *Coping With Suicide*, Sheldon Press, 1989
Sister Margaret Pennells and Susan C. Smith, *The Forgotten Mourners*, Jessica Kingsley, 1995
Ian Ainsworth-Smith and Peter Speck, *Letting Go*, SPCK, 1982
Barbara Ward, *Healing Grief*, Vermilion, 1993

Also available on cassette:

Dealing With Bereavement by Ursula Markham, available from: The Hypnothink Foundation, PO Box 66, Gloucester GL2 9YG

Other titles by Ursula Markham:

Alternative Health – Hypnosis, Optima, 1987
Creating a Positive Self-Image, Element Books, 1995
The Elements of Visualisation, Element Books, 1989
Helping Children Cope with Stress, Sheldon Press, 1990
How to Deal with Difficult People, Thorsons, 1993
How to Survive Without a Job, Piatkus, 1994

Hypnosis Regression Therapy, Piatkus, 1991
Life Scripts, Element Books, 1993
Living with Change, Element Books, 1993
Managing Stress, Element Books, 1995
Memory Power, Vermilion, 1993
Women and Guilt, Piatkus, 1995
Women Under Pressure, Element Books, 1990
Your Four-Point Plan for Life, Element Books, 1991

Useful Addresses

AUSTRALIA

Compassionate Friends:

9 Carlise Avenue
Morphettville 5043
Adelaide

79 Stirling Street
Perth
WA 6000
Tel: 09 370 3032

PO Box 218
Springwood
Queensland 4127
Tel: 07 252-7546

Bereaved Parents Support Centre
Lower Parish Hall
300 Camberwell Road
Camberwell 3124
Melbourne
Tel: 03-802 8222

Information and Drop-In Centre
13th Floor, 115 Pitt Street
Sydney 2000
NSW
Tel: 233 3731

Samaritan/Befrienders

60 Bagot Road
Subiaco
Perth
WA 6008
Tel: 61 93 81 5555

PO Box 991
Albany
WA 6330
Tel: 61 98 41 4777

Springwood Neighbourhood Centre
Macquarie Road
PO Box 161
Springwood
NSW 2777
Tel: 61 47 51 6402

PO Box 228
Launceston
Tasmania
Tel: 61 03 31 3355

SOUTH AFRICA

Compassionate Friends
PO Box 46305
Orange Grove
Johannesburg 2119
Tel: 011 887 9493
Fax: 011 887 9494

UK

British Association for Counselling
1 Regent Place
Rugby
Warwickshire CV21 2PJ
Tel: 01788 550899
They will provide the address of a counsellor in your area

Compassionate Friends
53 North Street
Bristol BS3 1EN
Tel: 0117 953 9639

Cruse
Cruse House
126 Sheen Road
Richmond
Surrey TW9 1UR
Tel: 0181 940 4818

Foresight Association
The Old Vicarage
Church Lane
Godalming
Surrey GU8 5PN
Tel: 01483 427839
For the promotion of preconceptual care

Foundation for Black Bereaved Families
11 Kingston Square
Salters Hill
London SE19 1DZ
Tel: 0181 761 7228

National Association of Bereavement Services
20 Norton Folgate
Bishopsgate
London E1 6DB
Tel: 0171 247 1080

Stillbirth & Neonatal Death Society
28 Portland Place
London WIN 3DE
0171 436 5881

Jewish Bereavement Counselling Service
126 Albert Street
London NW1 1NF
0171 267 6111

USA

Compassionate Friends

PO Box 3696
Oak Brook
Illinois 60522-3696
Tel: 312-990-0010

Samaritan Befrienders

PO Box 5228
Albany
NY 12205
Tel: 1 518 459 4040

500 Commonwealth Ave
Kenmore Square
Boston
MA 02215
Tel: 1 617 247 0220

386 Stanley Street
Fall River
MA 02720
Tel: 1 508 673 3777

PO Box 12004
Hartford
CT 06112
Tel: 1 203 232 2121

PO Box 832
Keene
NH 03431
Tel: 1 603 357 5505

2013 Elm Street
Manchester
NH 03404
Tel: 1 603 622 3836

2 Magee Street
Providence
RI 02906
Tel: 1 401 272 4044

PO Box 1259
New York
NY 10159
Tel: 1 212 673 3000

PO Box 9814
Washington
DC 20016
Tel: 1 202 362 8100

Index

ELEMENT BOOKS LTD
PUBLISHERS

Element is an independent general publishing house. Our list includes titles on Religion, Personal Development, Health, Native Traditions, Modern Thought and Current Affairs, and is probably the most comprehensive collection of books in its sphere.

To order direct from Element Books, or to join the Element Club without obligation and receive regular details of great offers, please contact:
Customer Services, Element Books Ltd, Longmead, Shaftesbury, Dorset SP7 8PL, England.   Tel: 01747 851339   Fax: 01747 851394

Or you can order direct from your nearest distributor:

UK and Ireland
Penguin Group Distribution Ltd,
Bath Road, Harmondsworth,
Middlesex UB7 0DA, England.
Tel: 0181 899 4000
Fax: 0181 899 4020/4030

Canada
Penguin Books Canada Ltd,
10 Alcorn Avenue, Suite 300,
Toronto, Ontario MV4 3B2.
Tel: (416) 925 2249
Fax: (416) 925 0068

Central & South America & the Caribbean
Humphrey Roberts Associates,
24 High Street,
London E11 2AQ, England.
Tel: 0181 530 5028
Fax: 0181 530 7870

USA
Viking Penguin Inc,
375 Hudson Street, New York,
NY 10014.
Tel: (212) 366 2000
Fax: (212) 366 2940

Australia
Jacaranda Wiley Ltd, PO Box
1226, Milton, Queensland 4064.
Tel: (7) 369 9755 Fax: (7) 369 9155

New Zealand
Forrester Books NZ Ltd,
3/3 Marken Place, Glenfield,
Auckland 10.
Tel: 444 1948   Fax: 444 8199

Other areas:
Penguin Paperback Export Sales,
27 Wrights Lane,
London W8 5TZ, England.
Tel: 0171 416 3000
Fax: 0171 416 3060

The Health Essentials Series

Comprehensive, high-quality introductions to complementary healthcare

Each book in the *Health Essentials* series is written by a practising expert in their field, and presents all the essential information on each therapy, explaining what it is and how it works. Advice is also given, where possible, on how to begin using the therapy at home, together with comprehensive lists of courses and classes available worldwide.

In this series:

Acupuncture, Peter Mole	ISBN 1 85230 319 0
The Alexander Technique, Richard Brennan	ISBN 1 85230 217 8
Aromatherapy, Christine Wildwood	ISBN 1 85230 216 X
Ayurveda, Scott Gerson	ISBN 1 85230 335 2
Chi Kung, James MacRitchie	ISBN 1 85230 371 9
Chinese Medicine, *Tom* Williams	ISBN 1 85230 589 4
Colour Therapy, Pauline Wills	ISBN 1 85230 364 6
Flower Remedies, Christine Wildwood	ISBN 1 85230 336 0
Herbal Medicine, Vicki Pitman	ISBN 1 85230 591 6
Kinesiology, Ann Holdway	ISBN 1 85230 433 2
Massage, Stewart Mitchell	ISBN 1 85230 386 7
Reflexology, Inge Dougans with Suzanne Ellis	ISBN 1 85230 218 6
Self-Hypnosis, Elaine Sheehan	ISBN 1 85230 639 4
Shiatsu, Elaine Liechti	ISBN 1 85230 318 2
Skin and Body Care, Sidra Shaukat	ISBN 1 85230 350 6
Spiritual Healing, Jack Angelo	ISBN 1 85230 219 4
Vitamin Guide, Hasnain Walji	ISBN 1 85230 375 1

128/144 pages • 216 x 138 mm • Paperback • Line illustrations
UK £5.99 • USA $9.95 • Canada $12.99